The Artist and the Trinity

The Artist and the Trinity

Dorothy L. Sayers' Theology of Work

Christine M. Fletcher

foreword by Malcolm Brown

PICKWICK *Publications* · Eugene, Oregon

THE ARTIST AND THE TRINITY
Dorothy L. Sayers' Theology of Work

Pickwick Publications
An Imprint of Wipf and Stock Publishers
199 W. 8th Ave., Suite 3
Eugene, OR 97401

www.wipfandstock.com

ISBN 13: 978-1-62032-375-5

Cataloging-in-Publication data:

Fletcher, Christine M.

The artist and the trinity : Dorothy L. Sayers' theology of work / Christine M. Fletcher ; foreword by Malcolm Brown.

xx + 142 p.; 23 cm—Includes bibliographical references and index.

ISBN 13: 978-1-62032-375-5

1. Sayers, Dorothy L. (Dorothy Leigh), 1893–1957—Criticism and interpretation. 2. Work—Religious aspects—Christianity. I. Brown, Malcolm, 1954–. II. Title.

BX5199.S267 F54 2013

Manufactured in the USA.

To Peter

Contents

Foreword by Malcolm Brown ix

Acknowledgments xiii

Introduction xv

1 Sayers' Life and Work 1

2 Imaginative Writing: Showing not Telling 16

3 Sayers' Wartime Writing 39

4 The Artist and the Trinity 70

5 Good Work 91

Appendix I: The Joint Letter on the Five Peace Points 123

Appendix II: Christ the Worker a Dogmatic Approach 125

Bibliography 127

Index 135

Foreword

WHEN CHRIS FLETCHER FIRST outlined to me her thinking about Dorothy L. Sayers' theology of work, I realised that I ought to reacquaint myself with an author who I had read only sketchily many years before. Continuing the discussion with Chris whilst simultaneously reading the Peter Wimsey novels, *The Mind of the Maker* and other pieces gave a fascinating insight into the integrity of a life. For Sayers, theology, art and life were inextricably woven together and were shaped inexorably by her experience as a woman and a lay Christian. All these factors coalesce in her exploration of the nature of human work.

A woman, a lay (Roman Catholic) Christian, with extensive experience of seeking to live faithfully through a diverse working life, Chris Fletcher understandably found a natural affinity with Sayers. But her study here goes a very long way beyond sympathetic affinity. Whilst Sayers' fiction occupies the "mental landscape" of the between-Wars period when detective stories were enjoying their classic period, Fletcher locates her, no less strongly, in the wartime and post-War period of reconstruction which was a similarly classic period for Anglican Social Theology. From the Malvern Conference of 1941, through the birth of the Welfare State and into an age when prosperity was forcing the pace of social and moral change, the Church of England was connecting with public policy in a way which was unprecedented in modern times and which still constitutes an almost mythical "golden age" for socially-aware Anglicans. Fletcher locates Sayers very firmly within that genre of Anglican social thinking and thereby helps us see further into the interdisciplinary nature of that movement, here shown to embrace art and literature as well as economics, political theory, social sciences and theology.

Although this book is, in one sense, "about" Dorothy L Sayers, it significance is theological rather than biographical. Since the mid-Twentieth Century, and the period when Anglican theology appeared to be shaping Britain's post-War reconstruction in many respects, it has generally been true that the church's commitment to social action remained whilst its grasp of the theological foundations for that action withered. William Temple's theological seriousness, and the deep philosophical, theological and social arguments that he and his associates (including Sayers) adduced for the church's social engagement, were largely forgotten as the Church of England tended to seek relevance in preference to theological authenticity. This lack of theological depth made it easy for the church to revert to an inward-looking pietism from the 1980s onwards which had little if anything to say about the Christian vision of a good society. By turning the spotlight on Sayers' contribution here, Fletcher shows how the theological seriousness of her period was not the preserve of bishops and clergy but could be, and was, integral to the reflections of a highly intelligent lay woman who saw very clearly how Christian faith could permeate the story of the world, humanity and the created order.

It is precisely this sense of a sublime and persuasive narrative of faith which has come back into fashion in contemporary theological movements such as Radical Orthodoxy. Owing much to the thinking of the Thomist moral philosopher, Alasdair MacIntyre, Radical Orthodoxy has presented itself as an emphatic break with the past traditions of Anglican social thought. Fletcher shows that the tradition within which Sayers, along with Temple, stood was far from being disconnected from elements of Catholic Social Teaching and, hence, a lineage can be constructed, through Aquinas and MacIntyre, between apparently very different theological movements. Again, the seriousness and depth of the Anglican tradition to which Sayers contributed is very apparent.

But this book is of contemporary, as well as historical, interest. Human labour is part of the experience of almost every Christian and yet it has too rarely been a focal theme for Christian ethics. Most of what has passed for a "theology of work" in the UK and USA has, until recently, had the character of personal anecdote linked, more or less adequately, to sermonic reflection. Secular commentators have begun to take an interest in work—not least, the persistence of soul-destroying labour and inhuman conditions in the most economically prosperous nations of all time. But if the problems around work are to be addressed, political ideology can only get one so far when unaccompanied by a more profound anthropology than secular managerialist theories can offer. Sayers was one of the few who tackled this theme. Perhaps, being a lay woman in a world where theology was the preserve of male clerics, she was one of the few with the courage and experience to do so. It remains that there have not been many who were willing or able to build on her theological reflections on work, and even what she did has largely been forgotten. Over fifty years after Sayers' death, Fletcher convincingly points us back to her anthropology and her grasp of how good work can mirror the divine nature. If this book can serve as a stimulus for new theological work about "work" – and new theology that will be duly cognisant of the resource which Sayers represents – it will have served the church and the academy well.

Working with Chris Fletcher on this project was not only intellectually exciting but a lot of fun—I hope for us both. We argued and shouted our way through hours of discussion, went back again and again to Sayers' books and enjoyed all the ecumenical tensions you would expect between a Roman Catholic and an Anglican post-liberal! I ended up with a much more profound respect for Sayers' contribution to Anglican social thought and some foundations for thinking further about the contemporary problems of work. Chris ended up with some more letters after her name and a challenging new job. You, the reader, end up with the work between these covers. I think it is original, timely and thought-provoking. I hope you do too.

Malcolm Brown
Director of Mission and Public Affairs
The Archbishops' Council of the Church of England
July 2012

Acknowledgments

MANY PEOPLE HELPED ME with this study and it is impossible to thank them adequately. I would like to mention especially Rev. Dr. Malcolm Brown and Fr. Aidan Nichols for their guidance and critiques throughout the project and Dr. Ann Loades for her support of this publication.

Many thanks to archivists at The Marion E. Wade Center at Wheaton College who are patient, knowledgeable and helpful.

Members of the Dorothy L. Sayers Society have been a constant source of expertise, advice and encouragement. I would like to mention especially Barbara Reynolds, Suzanne Bray, Bunty Parkinson, and the late Christopher Dean who did so much to encourage Sayers' scholarship.

Finally, I would like to thank my family for their constant support.
CMF

Introduction

"WHAT IS WOMAN'S WORK?" has been my core concern—as student, career woman, wife, mother, returning student and now college professor. Coming of age, as I did, in the early 1970s, in the heyday of what is now called Second Wave Feminism, I experienced the old certainties of social roles, including gender roles, being cast aside in the sweeping tide of the radical challenges of the liberation movements. A participant observer of the culture wars about motherhood and work, I want to review and clarify the gains that women have achieved, and identify what we have learned which can contribute to a better life for women and for men.

I write as someone who sees men and women struggling with balancing work and life. In a time of economic stress, this balance seems ever more elusive. Those who are employed are asked to work longer hours; those who are unemployed are facing a job market that looks for the cheapest labor, disregarding the need to pay a living wage with good benefits. We have seen manufacturing change, move off-shore, and the service economy provide more of the jobs. These jobs, though, are often low-wage, part-time employment lacking healthcare coverage or job security. The work itself is standardized in such a way that the workers need few skills; so they are interchangeable and need little training.

I decided to pursue theology as my work and studied a woman who had intrigued me through her mystery writing, especially the book *Gaudy Night*. In Dorothy L. Sayers (1893–1957) I found a woman who spent her life engaged with her faith intellectually, who was passionately concerned about good work and women's chance to use their talents.

She approached this question through her Christian faith, which made her an interesting voice. In the Mommy wars of the 1980s many Christians equated being a good mother with being a stay-at-home mother, as part of God's plan. Sayers offered an alternative vision which was based on the most basic doctrines of Christianity, the Incarnation and the Trinity. Her life-long fascination with the Athanasian Creed informed all of her writing: mysteries, drama, translations and essays. She saw that the doctrines of the Incarnation and the Trinity rightly understood and applied to life result in a respect for creation and human work, and ground human solidarity.

It may seem strange to use the writings of a woman from the early 20th century, writing about Christianity in Britain, to address the problem of good work in the global economy of the 21st century, but Sayers has something of importance to say to anyone interested in work as part of a fulfilling human life. She herself struggled to find employment, worked in an advertising agency, and finally as a free lance writer. She experienced the Great Depression, and saw the suffering of those who had no work. She was part of a great movement of Christians who wanted to create a social order that was more just, and participated in the great conversations of her day about work and society, economics and family life. She is a voice that is relevant today.

Sayers is best known for her mystery novels which feature Lord Peter Wimsey. Her novels have never been out of print and many have been turned into television plays. In 1930 she introduced a love interest for Wimsey: Harriet Vane, described as an Oxford educated writer whom Wimsey loves as much for her brain as for her appearance. Over several novels she explores Harriet and Peter's relationship; in *Gaudy Night* they finally agree to marry, and in *Busman's Honeymoon* we have a love story interrupted by a corpse, which gives Sayers a chance to show what love might mean to two intelligent people who hold an ideal of integrity and see marriage as a partnership of equals, each of whom has a role in the public and the private sphere.

Sayers focused on integrity in work throughout her life, as a young woman seeking a satisfactory career with a living wage that was not nursing or teaching, as a writer deciding which commissions to accept, and as a novelist and playwright. In her novels and plays she showed the conflict between the personal and the demands of integrity to work, whether scholarship, architecture or detecting. She was a writer who created narratives which displayed the truths and complexities of human lives, and showed women as human beings who needed to do good work for a satisfying life.

Through the war years she lectured and wrote on vocation in work and post-war reconstruction. Much of her work during the war has not been studied in depth, and as that was the period when she was concentrating on presenting her ideas about work and human life, it is a rich field to mine which adds to Sayers' studies as well as to social ethics.

She was a Christian whose Christianity was primarily expressed through her formidable intellect. She approached theology through narrative and writing in a way which pre-figures the concerns of modern theology about the relation of revelation, text and audience. In her radio plays *The Man Born to Be King*, she was one of the first to present the Gospel in a modern, naturalistic style which we today take for granted, but which caused an uproar at the time. In *The Mind of the Maker* she proposed an understanding of the human person as essentially creative, and therefore that work fit for humans should fit the Trinitarian creativeness of our being.

I am using the term theological anthropology for the conception of the person within a theological tradition. Sayers would not have used this term but would acknowledge that she was explaining one way that humanity bears the image of God. Her work as a writer of narrative and of theology within her conscious adherence to Christianity produced insights that we can now bring together as her theological anthropology. As a writer of narrative, she created characters and so investigated the depths of the human heart. As a writer and especially as a playwright, she experienced creation as a three-fold process which she examined in light of her understanding of the Christian doctrine of the Trinity. Her analogy appeared in its full form in the printed version of the play *The Zeal of Thy House* and was discussed in detail in her book *The Mind of the Maker* (see chapter 5).

From this analogy she has developed a theological understanding of human beings and their work. Sayers' perspective on work and gender emphasized equality, as the three persons in the one God are co-equal. She described men and women as humans, equal and more alike in their common humanity than they are distinctive in their genders. As male and female, they bear the image of the Trinitarian God in their ability to create. Sayers' account of good work is based on this anthropology and claims that differences between individual men or individual women are just as distinctive and important as the distinction between genders.

Sayers offers, I think, two major contributions to the ethical reasoning about work: first her Trinitarian anthropology of the person, and second, the ethics of work which develops from that anthropology. Sayers was not a professional theologian. In her own day, her work was read as apologetics not theology, but her methods are comparable to those theologians in our day, such as George Lindbeck[1] or Stanley Hauerwas, who recognise the fruitfulness of a methodology based on a mutual exchange between literature and theology.

Ann Loades, an Anglican theologian who has produced many works of interest especially on or about feminist theology, has produced several works based around Sayers. She believes Sayers offers resources we need now, as Sayers was committed to a sacramental understanding of the world.[2] This sacramental understanding of matter as good, is needed now more than ever, as the demands of the consumer economy create more and more environmental degradation.

A further problem with good work is that we systematically undervalue the work of care: compare a day-care worker's salary to a rookie professional athlete, a public relations consultant or a neophyte banker. No Christian account of work is complete without a full valuation of the care of the young, old, sick, and disabled. Sayers gives us a solid theological starting point for this valuation in her analogy of the Trinity, which is essentially social. She does not explicitly discuss the question of the work of care, for in her society the assignment of that work to women was almost unquestioned. In our day, though, we need a better understanding of the importance of the work of care not only to those who are in need of care, but to the full human development of all humans as care-givers. The great commandment, Love your neighbor as yourself, applies to everyone. Alasdair MacIntyre's work, *Dependent Rational Animals*, with its account of the family as a practice offers a philosophical basis for an ethics of care that isn't gender based. Together, MacIntrye and Sayers give us a theologically grounded account of work in a good human life.

---

1. Sayers' preface to the published version of *The Man Born to Be King* discusses the doctrine as the framework of her plays, controlling the characters and locking the dramatic action together in a way which foreshadows Lindbeck's *The Nature of Doctrine Religion and Theology in a Postliberal Age* (1984). Comparing the two in detail would be fruitful, but it is beyond the scope of this study.

2. Loades, *Feminist Theology Voices from the Past*, 170.

We possess an extended letter which gives us Sayers' perception of her task and method in theology. Sayers described what it is that "her sort" can safely do and categorised her own writings.

1. We can write a book, play or other work which genuinely and directly derives from such fragments of religious or human experience as we ourselves have (*The Zeal of Thy House* —the sin of the artist; *The Just Vengeance*—which is about the choosing of God through the only values we know). . . .

2. We can (if we feel like it) write a direct statement about our own experience. (*The Mind of the Maker*). . . .

3. We can *show you in images* [sic] experiences which we ourselves do not know, or know only imaginatively (*The Man Born to Be King*). Because in this, we do not need to pretend anything about ourselves. . . .

4. We can interpret another man, who has what we have not (we can translate and edit Dante). Our intellect can assess him and our imagination feels what he feels. . . .

5. We can, so far as our competence goes, help to disentangle the language-trouble by translating from one jargon to another. For this, we need to know both jargons thoroughly.[3]

In these five points she has categorized her writing over her lifetime. She does not include her detective fiction in her scheme, but I believe we can read her detective novels as narratives which show us the human values of work and of relationships grounded on equality. Her work as a playwright, a translator and a Christian apologist present a consistent theological ethic of work which is as applicable today as it was in the 1940s.

Plan of the Book

Chapter 1 discusses Sayers' life, highlighting some of the influences on her writing and showing her constant interest in the question of work and integrity. An overview of her lifetime of writing is given.

Chapter 2 looks at Sayers' narratives, the detective fiction and her plays. In terms of attracting readers, her detective novels are the most important. She is part of the Golden Age of detective fiction, was a serious student of the genre, and a craftsman who brought the detective story from a simple whodunit to a novel of manners. Her novels show us her vision of work as a necessary part of a fulfilling life for all human beings. In her

3. Sayers, *Letters Vol. 4*, 141–42.

detective fiction we find novels of social criticism that show us the importance of good work for men and for women, including for her hero, Lord Peter Wimsey. The plays are important because it was in her experience of the theater that her analogy for the Trinity came alive.

Chapter 3 discusses her war-time work, and will give a detailed account of Sayers' writings and speeches about work and vocation. The chapter will place Sayers in the Anglican Social Ethics of that period and highlight William Temple's influence in bringing Sayers to national prominence as a Christian thinker. The chapter aims to show what a significant national figure in the debate about social ethics and the post-war world Sayers was, and how her ideas are still relevant.

Chapter 4 explains the importance of Sayers' idea of human beings bearing the image of God in their ability to create. She created an analogy for the Trinity to the process of artistic creation. Her analogy to the Trinity brings that doctrine into the lived reality of Christian life, rescuing it from isolation in systematic theology by reconstructing social ethics on the need for men and women to live creatively in all areas of their lives. Her analogy is especially helpful to social ethics because it is not self-contained as Augustine's analogy of the human mind, but relational: the third term connects the person with other persons. From this analogy she develops her theological anthropology which understands the person as individual and essentially relational, thus accounting for particularity in Christian ethics without lapsing into an atomism of the individual of modern liberal capitalism.

Chapter 5 discusses Sayers' conception of good work which arises directly from her anthropology of person as creator. To fill out Sayers' account of good work, her writing is put into dialogue with Alasdair MacIntyre's idea of practices and their sustaining institutions and especially with MacIntyre's account of the family as a practice. This dialogue yields a human ethic of work that accounts for the interdependence of human beings, and the ethical requirements of caring for the weak, the young and the old that is gender neutral.

1

Sayers' Life and Work

DOROTHY L. SAYERS WAS a child of the vicarage. Her father, the Rev. Henry Sayers was headmaster of the choir school for Christ Church when she was born, when she was four years old, he accepted the living of Bluntisham-cum-Earith in Cambridgeshire. Her parents taught her at home and gave her a broader preparation than that typical for a girl intended for society and then marriage, perhaps the result of Henry Sayers' talents as school-master and enlightened outlook on female education. Her father developed her gifts, musical and intellectual. He taught her the violin and started her on Latin when she was six. She had French and German governesses. She remarked to Norah Lambourne while they were making paper maché props for the first production of *The Emperor Constantine*, that she didn't do crafts at home. She remembered her father saying "That's not for you, Dorothy."[1]

Her father seems not to have given her much explicit religious in-struction, but Dorothy grew up with household daily prayers and attended the services in the parish church, where she became "thoroughly familiar . . . with the Book of Common Prayer, and the rich and intellectually de-manding theology of Matins and Evensong and the Authorized Version of the Bible."[2] The language of the liturgy, especially the Athanasian Creed, made a deep impression on her that lasted all her life. In a letter to two Irish

1. Personal conversation with Norah Lambourne at the Dorothy L. Sayers' Society Convention, 2001.

2. Loades, *Feminist Theology*, 170.

clergymen she reminisced about how much she looked forward to reciting that creed, even though she couldn't understand it, "but it was grand. So mysterious and full of rumbling great worlds, and it made such a wonderful woven pattern. And it didn't talk down to me[.]"[3]

She was surrounded by books and pursued her interests with great zest, and with a mind that constantly sought for connections between the content of her studies. She later recounted how excited she was to find that geometry really worked, in marking out the tennis court, or the thrill when she realized that Ahasuerus, a Bible person, was Xerxes. This connection showed her how she had two spheres: the Bible, stained glass, and history, factual and interesting. This insight informed how she conceived her task as a Christian writer.[4]

Neither Sayers or her parents were willing to have her life defined by the gender roles of her time. The Sayers raised their daughter to focus on using her talents. They hoped that she would attend one of the new colleges for women, and to that end they sent her to the Godolphin School. It is consistent with their liberality in her upbringing, and her aunt's example, that she sat for a scholarship to Somerville, the non-sectarian women's college. She succeeded in winning the Gilchrist Scholarship at Somerville College, read Modern Languages with Mildred Pope and took a First in her examinations in 1915.

At Somerville she and several kindred spirits, Dorothy Rowe, Amphilis Middlemore, Margaret Chub and Claris Frankenberg, arranged weekly meetings to read aloud their literary efforts. Their name, bestowed by Sayers, was The Mutual Admiration Society (MAS), since that is what college would have called them anyway. Her interest in Christianity and Christian themes was reflected in her writing for the Society. Claris Frankenberg remembered that Dorothy Sayers read a conversation between the three Magi. A short story from the group's magazine of 1917, "Who Calls the Tune?" attempts to portray what happens when a man dies and faces judgment.

Her letters from Oxford show a normal young woman enjoying friendships with men and women and comfortable with following fashion, "On Friday Aunt Maud took me to Elliston's to choose the evening cloak . . . I have made myself the most ravishing little cap to wear in New College chapel—on the model of the one Gladys sent me. It is executed in black

3. Sayers, *Letters Vol. 2*, 154.

4. See Reynolds, *Dorothy L. Sayers*, 30, for the account of marking out the tennis court, and Sayers, *Unpopular Opinions*, 24, for the Ahasuerus reference.

ribbon and net, and is so becoming, the Bursar thinks it is quite unsuitable for a place of worship!"[5] She attended church services regularly, and was reading the Gospel. A letter to her parents foreshadows her work on *The Man Born to Be King*, "Having read the two Gospels with more attention than I had ever before given to the subject, I came to the conclusion that such a set of stupid, literal, pig-headed people never existed as Christ had to do with, including the disciples."[6] She wrote to her parents about her spiritual journey:

> It isn't a case of "here is the Christian religion, the one authoritative and respectable rule of life. Take it or leave it". It's "here's a muddling kind of affair called Life, and here are nineteen or twenty different explanations of it, all supported by people whose opinions are not to be sneezed at. Among them is the Christian religion in which you happen to have been brought up. Your friend so-and-so has been brought up in quite a different way of thinking; is a perfectly splendid person and thoroughly happy. What are you going to do about it?"—I'm worrying it out quietly, and whatever I get hold of will be valuable because I've got it for myself.[7]

Her intellectual interest in Christianity continued, and G. K. Chesterton was an influence. She reported buying his *What's Wrong with the World*, a book she recommended to her parents.[8] She commented to a friend that the Christian Union is all wrong, "Christianity rests on Faith, not Faith on Christianity. If you have read *Orthodoxy* you will see what I mean."[9] In May and again in June of 1914 she heard Chesterton speak and was most impressed with his wit and manner, which was not as aggressive as his prose would lead one to believe. On Chesterton's death in 1936, she wrote in a letter of condolence to Mrs. Chesterton, "I think, in some ways, G. K.'s books have become more a part of my mental make-up than those of any writer you could name."[10]

She was thoroughly happy at Oxford, with an active social life and a satisfying intellectual life. She wanted a life which would include a satisfying personal life and the kind of literary work that had made her time there

---

5. Sayers, *Letters Vol. 1*, 86.

6. Ibid., 71.

7. Ibid., 85.

8. Ibid., 71.

9. Ibid., 72.

10. Ibid., 394.

so happy. Initially, she taught in a girls' school in Hull, which she found unsatisfying. She returned to Oxford to work for Basil Blackwell, her father paying Blackwell £100 per annum for having Sayers as an apprentice. While she was learning the publishing trade she published two volumes of poetry, *Op I* (1916) and *Catholic Tales and Christian Songs* (1918). These volumes expressed her faith in ways that reviewers found new and refreshing, and one of the poems, "When All the Saints" was set to music by Henry Ley, then organist at Christ Church.[11]

During this period she had a number of difficulties with social relationships which she made light of in her letters home, but provoked her to write an essay "Eros in Academe" which appeared in 1919 in *The Oxford Outlook*. This lamented that educated women in her time no longer have the social skills that the educated women of the Middle Ages and the Renaissance had. She placed much of the blame on the patterning of female education upon that of men's education. She pointed out that women mature earlier; a man leaves university, "still a lad, and can go and find knowledge where and how he pleases; the girl when she goes down is already a woman and if she is still socially ignorant it is late for her to begin learning. . . . They [women] cannot grow wise in an atmosphere in which going to tea with a youth ranks as a thrilling dissipation."[12]

Sayers was never prepared to accept the safety of marriage if the marriage she was offered was not a passionate, equal partnership. While at Blackwell's, she had acquired a serious admirer in the Rev. Leonard Hodgson, later Regius Professor of Divinity at Oxford, but she found his devotion distasteful.[13] She fell in love with Eric Whelpton, an ex-officer who was trying to finish his degree, and seems to have been more attracted to him than he to her. When he decided to move to France to run an agency for exchange students, Dorothy followed him as his secretary. At this time she was devouring the Sexton Blake books with an eye to supporting herself by writing detective stories. Whelpton was critical of this ambition. Nevertheless she continued reading and trying to write them. When he moved back to London and ended their relationship, she, too, returned to London.

She was writing her first detective novel and tried supply teaching, coaching and translating to tide her over while she tried to find a publisher. She realised she was a drain on her parents, but wanted to be independent

11. Ibid., 145–46.
12. Sayers, "Eros," 114–15.
13. Reynolds, *Dorothy L. Sayers*, 96–97.

and not return to live in the vicarage, a surplus woman like her aunts. When in London she lamented to her parents, "I can't get the work I want, not the money I want, nor (consequently) the clothes I want, nor the holiday I want, nor the man I want!!"[14] I think it is significant that she wanted both the work and the man, but the work came first in the litany. In 1922 she was taken on as a copywriter at S. H. Benson's Advertising Agency, and found professional and financial stability, writing advertising copy in the day and detective novels in the evening. *Whose Body?,* her first detective novel, came out in 1923. It featured her hero, Lord Peter Wimsey, who is discussed in more detail in the following chapter.

Sayers' time at Bensons coincided with the beginning of the modern agency system as we know it. It was a period of remarkable growth in advertising. She worked for Oswald Greene, a director of the agency and one of its best copy writers. He believed in "reason why" copy and was famous for the campaigns Benson's created for Coleman's Mustard (The Mustard Club) and for Guinness. Sayers seems to have fit in easily from her accounts in her letters to her parents, "The office is always an amusement—I was really wonderfully lucky to get a job that suited me so well."[15] Sayers was a very successful copywriter whose career at Benson's could have continued were it not for her choice to retire from advertising to write full time in 1930.

In her early years at Bensons she was involved with John Cournos, for whom she cared deeply. She had the strength of mind to refuse a sexual relationship. He wanted her to use birth control and she refused.[16] When that relationship ended she took up with William White, for whom she cared very little. She had a sexual relationship with him and did use contraception but she became pregnant. She wrote to Cournos about this and explained that "the one thing worse than bearing the child of a man you hate would be being condemned to be childless by the man you loved. . . . when I see men callously and cheerfully denying women the full use of their bodies, while insisting with sobs and howls on the satisfaction of their own, I simply can't find it heroic or kind, or anything but pretty rotten and feeble."[17] She took a six week break from Bensons to have the baby, her son John Anthony, and complete her second mystery novel, *Clouds of Witness*

14. Sayers, *Letters Vol. 1,* 178.

15. Ibid., 197.

16. See Reynolds, *Sayers,* ch. 7 and Brabazon, *Sayers,* ch. 9.

17. Sayers, *Letters Vol. 1,* 217.

(1926). It was a period of great stress, yet she continued to work as a copy-writer and a mystery writer, and the work provided not only the financial support but also a relief to the emotional storms of her love for and rejection by Cournos. She placed her son with her cousin Ivy Shrimpton who fostered children professionally, and determined to keep his existence a secret from her parents and more particularly from her maiden aunts.

In 1926 she married Oswald Arthur Fleming, "Mac," a divorced veteran of World War I. She hoped that eventually she would be able to bring her son to live with them, a hope that was never realised. *Unnatural Death* (1927) and *The Unpleasantness at the Bellona Club* (1928) appeared adding to her reputation as a mystery writer. Her translation of *Tristan in Brittany*, begun while she was studying with Mildred Pope, was published in 1929.

On 20th September 1928 her father died, aged seventy-four. He had lived to see the beginnings of her success. Mac helped Mrs. Sayers sort out the rectory while Dorothy returned to work. Mac found a house in Witham, Essex, which became the home for Mrs. Sayers and Aunt Mabel. In June 1929, Mrs. Sayers died. By 1930 Sayers had achieved enough success as a mystery novelist to give up her job at Bensons. She and Mac moved to the house in Witham, with Aunt Mabel, although they kept the flat in Bloomsbury. She supported herself, Mac, John Anthony and Aunt Mabel with her writing. Her marriage, initially at least, must have been emotionally and physically satisfying for her according to her biographers.[18] The later years were difficult; Mac resented her success even though she was supporting them. During the Witham years, her private life was hidden from public view. She wanted people to look at her work and not at her personal life: the work she produced was important, not the personal or psychological details of her own existence.

In the early 1930s she published more novels featuring Wimsey: *Strong Poison* (1930), *The Five Red Herrings* (1931), *Have His Carcase* (1932) *Murder Must Advertise* (1933), *The Nine Tailors* (1934) *Gaudy Night* (1935), and *Busman's Honeymoon* (the play in 1936, the novel in 1937).

In addition to the Wimsey novels, in 1930 she wrote *The Documents in the Case* in collaboration with Robert Eustace, an epistolary novel without a central character who is the detective; that is left to the reader. She also released collections of short stories, *Lord Peter Views the Body*, (1928), *Hangman's Holiday* (1933) and *In the Teeth of the Evidence* (1939). She

18. Brabazon describes the early years of their marriage as "a time of pride and happiness." Brabazon, *Sayers*, 134.

edited three volumes of *Great Short Stories of Detection, Mystery and Horror* (1928, 1931 and 1934); her introductions are considered classics in literary criticism of the genre. She reviewed mysteries for *The Sunday Times* from June 1933 until August 1935. She helped found the Detection Club and took part in the joint novels the members wrote to finance the Club.

In the mid-1930s Sayers began working in the theatre, which gave her a respite from her difficult domestic situation, and a working life which she found exhilarating. She found herself in a new world, as Barbara Reynolds relates: "'There was I,' she once said to me, talking about this period of her life, 'stiff in my ways with strangers, suddenly plunged among people who called each other "darling" at first sight and immediately embraced without the slightest embarrassment.' She loved it and responded warmly."[19] Her first play was *Busman's Honeymoon*.

Before her play *Busman's Honeymoon* opened in London, Miss Babington of the Canterbury Festival committee wrote to Sayers asking her to do a play for the festival, at the suggestion, it is thought, of Charles Williams, who had written the play for the 1936 Festival.[20] Sayers initially refused, but changed her mind when she learned that the 1937 festival was to have the theme of Arts and Crafts. She wrote *The Zeal of Thy House* which opened in June 1937. The play gives the first statement of her analogy to the Trinity. This speech was cut from the performance but restored in the printed version of the play. It was read by Father Herbert Hamilton Kelly who wrote to Sayers asking, "I wonder if you recognize, or are interested in recognizing, how closely your book images the principles of the Athanasian Creed—the two-fold necessity of faith in the Trinity of God, and the Incarnation."[21] This inspired a correspondence which becomes the substance for Sayers' articles in the press on Christianity as well as *The Mind of the Maker* (1941), Sayers' major work of Trinitarian theology which is discussed in chapter 4.

The play moved to the West End after the short run in Canterbury. Sayers' talent for publicity and her desire to attract a general audience to the play led her to give press interviews in which she opined that the play was about Christian dogma. This was a startling statement. *The Sunday Times* commissioned an article to explain it. Sayers became an apologist for Christianity. Her work in this area is detailed in chapter 3.

19. Reynolds, *Sayers*, 302.

20. Ibid., 310.

21. Sayers, *Letters Vol. 2*, 42.

In "The Greatest Drama," the article for *The Sunday Times*, she made clear why the creeds' insistence of Jesus being fully man and fully God mattered:

> So that is the outline of the official story—the tale of the time when God was the under-dog and got beaten, when He submitted to the conditions He had laid down and became a man like the men He had made, and the men He had made broke Him and killed Him. . . . So they did away with God in the name of peace and quietness.
>
> "*And the third day He rose again*"; . . . One thing is certain: if He was God and nothing else, His immortality means nothing to us; if He was man and no more, His death is no more important to us than yours or mine. But if He really was both God and man, then when the man Jesus died, God died too, and when the God Jesus rose from the dead, man rose too, because they were one and the same person.[22]

In all her articles she saw herself not as being original but as using her skill as a craftsman in words to clarify the dogma of the Church. This dogma was an explanation of the universe that the public was free to accept or reject; her job was to make sure they understood exactly what they were usually rejecting without thought. The central dogma she defended was the Incarnation, that Christ was truly man and truly God. She later wrote, "It is only with the confident assertion of the creative divinity of the Son that the doctrine of the Incarnation becomes a real revelation of the structure of the world."[23]

The articles attracted the notice of Rev. F. A. Iremonger, then head of the BBC's religion department. He commissioned a nativity play from her which gave her an even wider audience. She wrote *He That Should Come*, a realistic play set in a bustling inn which used modern language. This is the first venture she made into treating the Gospels with the vividness and reality she had used in her apologetic writing. By not using the words of the Authorized Version she caused great offence. She publicised the play with an article in *Radio Times* with no apology for her use of modern language: "Give such a story actuality, and the result may appear startling, perhaps dangerous, possibly even blasphemous."[24] The play provoked a great

22. Ibid., 3–4.
23. Sayers, *Creed*, 38.
24. Sayers, "Nativity Play," 13.

response; Reynolds writes that the response "gave Dorothy a new view of herself and of her role as a writer. She experienced an increase in confidence and a surge of creative power."[25]

The theme of personal responsibility is central to Sayers' wartime writing. Her publisher, Victor Gollancz asked her to write a Christmas message to the nation. Instead of yet another Nativity meditation, or an uplifting pamphlet, which is probably what he had in mind, she responded with a book *Begin Here* (1939). She was asked to write another play for the Canterbury Festival and re-worked the Faust theme in *The Devil to Pay*. She had written a light-hearted play, *Love All*, in 1938 on the question of men and women and work. It had a short run in 1940 and received good reviews.

Sayers' spent the war giving speeches, usually on vocation in work, talks to the armed forces, broadcasting for the BBC, writing books, newspaper and magazine articles on a variety of topics, but mostly on the importance of personal responsibility and integrity in work. Her two outstanding achievements in theology were the play cycle, *The Man Born to be King*, (1941–1943) and the book *The Mind of the Maker* (1941). *The Man Born to be King* is written as a twelve-play series and can be read as a work of narrative theology. Before she had the opportunity to write the radio plays, she had written that "I believe one could find no better road to a realistic theology than that of coaching an intelligent actor to play the Leading Part [Christ] in the world's drama."[26] When the essay was published in the collection in 1947 she noted that she had been given that opportunity and "the reception given to *The Man Born to Be King* showed, I think, that the public thought it well worth trying."[27]

The Mind of the Maker summarizes her insights about work and bases them on an analogy to the Trinity in the work of the creative artist. This, however, was only a small part of the work she undertook in the following years. Her religious theatrical work led to her commissions for speeches on Christianity, work which demanded more and more of her time through the war years. She found the trips away from Witham a relief. The war years were some of the busiest in Sayers' life, and her writings and speeches of this period will be detailed in chapter 4.

Her Christian faith sustained her through her life, and found expression in all her works, the novels and plays as well as in the explicitly

25. Reynolds, *Sayers*, 327.

26. Sayers, *Unpopular Opinions*, 21.

27. Ibid., 23.

religious work. Though she was a public apologist for Christianity, Sayers was not an active churchwoman. She became friends with Fr. Patrick McLaughlin, a priest she knew through the Catholic Writers Guild. When Fr. McLaughlin and Fr. Gilbert Shaw founded their mission to intellectuals at St Anne's, Soho, Sayers helped by speaking, writing, and, in November 1944, becoming part of the Advisory Council, and eventually its chairman. She struggled to keep St Anne's alive and efficient. James Brabazon, her official biographer first saw and heard her at the mission at St Anne's in 1943. He writes: "There is little doubt that, but for her efforts, combined with the weight that her name still carried in the upper echelons of the Church of England, the St. Anne's experiment would have perished much sooner than it actually did."[28]

St Anne's was the only Church organisation in which Sayers took a sustained active role. She was not part of Dr. Oldham's Moot in Cambridge, or, despite some mistaken reports, of the Inklings. She worked on her writing in Witham, and maintained her professional relationships primarily by letter. Meetings with others, such as her producers, were arranged at the London flat when she was in town.

She read Charles Williams' *The Figure of Beatrice* when it appeared in August of 1943 and it inspired her to pick up her copy of Dante's *Divine Comedy* (which she thought had belonged to her grandmother) for reading when a doodlebug raid meant she had to retreat to the air-raid shelter. This was a road-to-Damascus experience; her entire life changed. From that point, 1944, until her death, the majority of her time and energy were focussed on her translation of *The Divine Comedy*. She wrote to the Bishop of St Alban that she found translation a good job for difficult days, "because I can take it away, a terzain at a time, and mull it over while I peel the potatoes or get on with the cooking. My husband always enjoys telling people how he came into the kitchen one evening and found me 'reciting Dante to the duck.'"[29] Mac was so difficult at times that she was forced to write late at night. Mac's health continued to deteriorate; he died in June, 1950. Sayers continued in the Witham house until her death in 1957.

From 1944 until her death in 1957 she worked on her translations of *The Divine Comedy*: *Hell* appeared in 1948, *Purgatory* in 1949, and *Paradise*, which was completed by Barbara Reynolds, in 1962. As a break from Dante, she translated *The Song of Roland* which appeared in 1956. In her

28. Brabazon, *Sayers*, 242.
29. Sayers, *Letters Vol. 3*, 406.

translation of *The Divine Comedy,* particularly in the introductions and notes, she demonstrated her ability to make a classic available to a public who is literate but not educated.

She was commissioned for two further religious plays, *The Just Vengeance,* 1946, and *The Emperor Constantine,* 1951. *The Just Vengeance,* which Sayers considered her finest work, was commissioned for Litchfield Cathedral Festival. It shows the influence of Sayers' work on Dante, and once again returns to the figure of Christ, and what human beings make of him, how we try to make him in our image. The final scenes of the play have the Persona Dei (the Lord Chancellor still did not allow Christ to appear on stage), in procession with the line, "He who carries the Cross, the Cross shall carry him."[30] *The Emperor Constantine* was written for the Colchester Festival, and is notable for a scene set at the Council of Nicea where the bishops are debating the nature of Christ. In both works, Sayers' mature thought as a Christian is displayed. The dramas deal with the theology of the atonement, and only indirectly with vocation in work.

The translation of Dante and her lecturing at the Summer School of Italian resulted in two volumes: *Introductory Papers on Dante* (1954) and *Further Papers on Dante* (1957), as well as a posthumous work of collected writings *The Poetry of Search and the Poetry of Statement* (1963). The works in these volumes which cover technical matters of translation and those which focus solely on literary criticism generally stand outside the scope of this study. The more philosophical papers which show her deep understanding of language, are relevant to judging her as a theologian and ethicist whose method was translation.

The two major events in her personal life, her son and her marriage, along with the unhappy experiences with Whelpton and Cournos give a quality to her writing that may be characterised as generosity. She knew she was a sinner by all her Church taught, and remained faithful. She never confused Christianity with respectability. In her detective novels she treats the realities of unplanned pregnancies, sexual desire and marital discontent with realism and a clear-eyed charity. Human lives are this messy and problematic. She neither forgot nor ignored the importance of erotic love; but she never exalted it into the primary concern in life. From her university days, she was aware of problems of educated women trying to relate to men. In "Eros in Academe" she laments the attitudes she found in her day, "We may hymn the flesh in attitudinising raptures in a public debate, but

30. Sayers, *Four Sacred Plays,* 344.

the one thing we must not—the one thing we seemingly cannot—do is to be cheerful and take it for granted."[31] It was an insight which speaks of the power of *eros* in life and in art; and one which has echoes throughout her writing. In her first religious play, *The Zeal of thy House*, the protagonist is a man of sensual habits conducting an illicit affair with the Lady Ursula. He is condemned not for his Lust, though that is recognized as a sin, but for his Pride in his craftsmanship. It is his work, however, that stands to his credit with God.

Sayers own life was described by her official biographer, Brabazon, as convincing her that "no trust could be placed in personal matters; that the only salvation came through work, through craftsmanship, through the creations of mind and of hand and through intellectual passion that controlled those creations."[32] This is a revealing quote for it displays Sayers' rejection of and Brabazon's attachment to the conventional woman's narrative in which only the personal provides meaning in life, and other work or interests are at best a compensation for lack of success in the personal sphere. Throughout Brabazon's biography he places Sayers' professional achievements as compensations for her failures in her love life. Although Sayers was unhappy in love, and did find professional life more rewarding, she perceived herself as failing in love because she didn't care enough about personal relationships.

Carolyn Heilbrun in *Writing a Woman's Life* has a different view of Sayers' life, "I believe Sayers's life to be an excellent example of a woman's unconscious 'fall' into a condition where vocation is possible and out of the marriage plot that demands not only that a woman marry but that the marriage and its progeny be her life's absolute and only center."[33] In Sayers' fiction the restriction of women's concerns to their partner and the home is shown to be unhealthy, a perversion of true love. This erotic plot is too narrow for any human being to live exclusively and live well.

Sayers' view of men, women, romance, marriage and work arises from her Christian faith and from her study of the literature of the Courts of Love. We can frame her output of novels, plays and essays with the essay "Eros in Academe" written at the beginning of her adult life in 1919 and her translation of the *Purgatory* of the Divine Comedy written towards the end of her life in 1955. In "Eros in Academe" she laments that she and her

31. Sayers, "Eros", 111.
32. Brabazon, *Sayers*, 151.
33. Heilbrun, *Writing*, 51.

friends talk about only one subject, but lack the wise leadership of Oisille or Parlamente. Those ladies were "the pick of the country's [Navarre's] brains . . . well dressed, witty, courteous, shrewd and could look on a man reasonably as a human being and not as a cataclysm of nature."[34] In the 1500s, women ruled the men without any political privilege; today, Sayers laments, we have political privilege, and women still rule men, but it is not the educated women who so rule. This, she says, "is bad for learning and worse for the world."[35] What Sayers particularly admires in Margaret of Navarre is her combination of wisdom with her mysticism: she knew that keeping a high ethical standard required worldly wisdom. It is the innocents who can be easily duped and betrayed.

In 1929 she published her translation of *Tristan in Brittany*. In her introduction she writes that the poet, Thomas was not really interested in the dragons, giants and magical marvels, but in the psychology of love. Sayers defines his conception of the passion of love as "a kind of half-way house between the old feudal morality and new and artificial 'amour courtois' . . . The beloved woman is no longer a chattel; but she has not yet become a cult."[36]

In 1955 she described the poetic doctrine of Courtly Love in the preface to *Purgatory*, in order to explain the relationship between Beatrice and Dante. First of all, it did not represent an attitude to sex, and it did not directly determine a man's behaviour to his wife. It was about the man's humility before his beloved, his "Madonna": he took orders from her. His wife and daughters took orders from him. The key for Sayers is that, "the doctrine of Courtly Love is so far realistic that it assigns all the amorous fuss and to-do, all the tormented philosophy of love, to the male" at least in theory. "It may be death to him, but to her it is a pastime."[37] This is the clearest contrast to the idea of women living only for love, a sentiment Sayers calls a piece of male wishful thinking, "Lovers, husbands, children, households—these are major feminine preoccupations: but not love."[38] She assigns all of the following to masculine inventiveness: the great love lyrics, the great love-tragedies, the romantic agony, the religion of beauty, the cult

---

34. Sayers, "Eros," 111.
35. Ibid., 111.
36. Sayers, *Tristam*, xxx.
37. Sayers, *Purgatory*, 32–33.
38. Ibid., 33.

of the *ewig Weibliches*, the exaltation of virginity, the worship of the dark Eros, the deification of motherhood, the Fatal Man and the Fatal Woman.[39]

Sayers' understanding of courtly love when combined with the Christian doctrine of Incarnation yields the marriage of Wimsey and Vane: the ideal marriage of minds and hearts as equals. Before she achieved that in her novels, she explored love as it existed in her day, good and bad, in marriages as well as in irregular unions. From the first to the last novel, and in most of the short stories, Sayers contrasts the conventional with the moral. Work and vocation are either major or minor themes in every novel, interwoven with the themes of the role of women in the society and marriage; this sets Sayers apart from Agatha Christie, who is content to accept the social norms of the day as the background of her mysteries.

Sayers knew joy through her work throughout her life. As a child, her writing and the enthusiastic participation of the household in her plays alleviated her loneliness. Throughout her unhappy experiences of love and marriage, work provided sustenance, an outlet, and an escape from the pressures of the personal. She made a living as a writer and negotiated the issues of writing for money, and being true to her writer's conscience. She did not pander to audiences. She chose detective fiction because it paid, but she wrote it with the intention of writing good fiction.

Her Christian faith influenced her life and all of her writings, even though only some of them were overtly theological. The figure of Christ exercised an intellectual and imaginative hold over her, witness her second book of poems, *Catholic Tales and Christian Songs*, her play-cycle, *The Man Born to Be King*, her apologetic writing on the Incarnation in her wartime work, and her plays *The Just Vengeance* and *The Emperor Constantine*. Because Christ was fully man and fully God, she held a sacramental view of the universe which meant that integrity in work mattered.

In *Creed or Chaos?* she noted that most people believe that for Christians matter and the body are evil; "But so long as the Church continues to teach the manhood of God and to celebrate the sacraments of the Eucharist and of marriage, no living man should dare to say that matter and the body are not sacred to her."[40] She saw the material world as "an expression and incarnation of the creative energy of God, as a book or a picture is the material expression of the creative soul of the artist."[41] This is the vision

---

39. Ibid., 33–34.
40. Sayers, *Creed*, 43.
41. Ibid.

that unifies her theology of work: the Incarnation which reveals matter as sacramental, that is, a sign of God; the Trinity which is a doctrine which can be partially understood by an analogy to the mind of a creative artist; and the importance of integrity in work, and secular work as the vocation of the lay Christian.

Her discernment of her own experiences and her observation of those around her gave her a depth of understanding of the evil inherent in the good we do, and that the good is never completely overcome by evil. This understanding is brought out especially in her novel *The Nine Tailors* and in her religious drama. She would bring this aspect of the created world out clearly in *The Mind of the Maker* and other works, and it informed her views on politics and international relations so that although an English patriot, she was never jingoistic. She knew that the solidarity in guilt applied to all human beings.

The Man Born to Be King and *The Mind of the Maker* are Sayers' major theological works, the first exploring Christology in a form of radio drama, a constraint that no academic theologian would attempt. *The Mind of the Maker* is closer to a work of propositional theology, but the analogy she proposes is new and illuminating. Her major concern, throughout both works, was to relate the doctrines of the Incarnation and the Trinity to the life of the individual particularly in his or her work. Chapter 3 provides a survey of Sayers' wartime works, which have received less attention than her novels, to demonstrate the unity and consistency of her theology and the development in it as she tested her ideas in various genres, and before various audiences in the context of a world on the brink of war, a nation standing alone against the Nazi threat, and a world coming to terms with the Holocaust and the Atom Bomb.

Her detective fiction, her first publications and still the most popular and well-known of her works, illustrate her ideas about the place of work and romance in life, and show us Sayers' moral framework which formed the basis for her later writing. Her experience writing plays made her analogy of creativity come alive. These narratives will be examined in the following chapter.

2

Imaginative Writing:
Showing not Telling

JILL PATON WALSH, IN a lecture titled "The Immortal Lord Peter," remarked that she pictured Sayers arriving in heaven and being comforted on the continued success of her detective stories and the neglect of her more serious work by Sir Arthur Sullivan, who couldn't get the angels to stop humming *The Mikado* and sing one of his oratorios.

I propose to read Sayers' detective stories as fiction which discloses her theology of work: meaningful work is important for men as for women, and that work should be suited to the workers' talents, not defined by their gender. It was in her detective fiction, and particularly in the novel *Murder Must Advertise*, that Sayers first showed us her analogy for the Trinity on which she based her ideas about good work. The theological ideas in the detective stories were developed more fully in her first Canterbury play, *The Zeal of Thy House*. Her essays and speeches from the war years, discussed in the next chapter, build on and explain these theological themes.

Sayers came of age when fiction for the masses and not for the elites was written to meet the needs of the newly literate population. From the 1880s onward a vast new pool of readers was created by universal elementary education. In the early years of the literacy boom, popular fiction was moral fiction, not as Sayers conceived it, but as a replacement for the religious tract. Writers coated the message of their moral and social agenda—temperance, fidelity to the family, manliness, femininity—in a story. Sayers, following R. G. Collingwood, characterized this type of writing as manipulative: "As the amusement-art seeks to produce the emotions without the experience, so this pseudo-art seeks to produce the behaviour without the experience. In the end it is directed to putting the behaviour of the audience beneath the will of the spell-binder and its true name is not 'art' but 'art-magic'. In its vulgarest form it becomes pure propaganda" [1]

Detective fiction is an amusement that may become something more. It presents the reader with a puzzle to solve, and has its own rules of fair play. The plots turn on the vices: greed, jealousy, envy, and hatred. The innocent are vindicated and the guilty punished. Sayers appreciated this point: "Do you realise that, as a class, we are the only novelists who have ever really succeeded in making the virtuous characters more interesting than the wicked ones? From that point of view, Conan Doyle is a much better influence than Milton. Satan is undoubtedly the hero of *Paradise Lost*, but Sherlock Holmes is not merely more virtuous but infinitely more interesting and exciting than Professor Moriarty." [2]

Sayers' detective novels are enduringly popular; they have never been out of print. Hodder and Stoughton brought out new editions of all the novels in 2004 and 2005. The editor of the series commented that the now general knowledge of Sayers' illegitimate son seems to have helped sales. She speculated that it removed the perception of Sayers as a religious prig. Sayers wanted to write them because they paid well. As a girl she was entranced by *The Three Musketeers*[3] with its masking and unmasking, confrontations, spying, the final trapping of the criminal and exposition of the complexities of the story. It is a detective story as well as an adventure story and a romance, and its influence, I think, can be seen in Sayers' choice of detective fiction rather than romantic fiction, which could have provided her a living, as it did for so many of her contemporaries. Her choice of detective fiction puts her own intellectual love of puzzles to use in creating the plots of her novels. As a genre detective fiction offered the writer greater creative possibilities than romance novels.

Her mysteries are not simple whodunits, but show her development as a novelist. Catherine Kenney remarks: "Sayers' religious convictions were implied in her fictional world from the beginning, becoming more

---

1. Sayers, *Unpopular Opinions*, 41.

2. Sayers, "Trials and Sorrows," 26.

3. See Reynolds, *Sayers*, 33.

patent as time passed"[4] Sayers viewed herself as a craftsman whose tool was language and approached detective fiction with that attitude. She wrote numerous articles about it, including "Aristotle and Detective Fiction" which discusses the art of misleading the readers while playing fair with them. When she was asked to contribute an article for the book *Titles to Fame* about her work, she obliged with a discussion of *Gaudy Night* in particular and her detective fiction in general. Her goal, she claimed, was that once again the detective novel would become a novel of manners as it had been in the hands of LeFanu and Collins.

In most of her fiction and her plays *Busman's Honeymoon* and *Love All,* we do not have much explicitly religious writing; there is however, an implicit view of justice and the complicity in guilt with humans share living in a community. Further, they display her ideas on the importance of good work for a fulfilling human life. She was not satisfied with the gender stereotypes of her day; her fiction shows an alternative. Her hero was Lord Peter Wimsey, second son of the Duke of Denver. The romantic interest she created was Harriet Vane, an Oxford educated doctor's daughter who turned to detective fiction to make ends meet.

Sayers wrote about love and marriage daring to take an unconventional line, and developing the theme of love in unexpected ways. She did not allow Harriet Vane to fall into Lord Peter's arms until she was his equal, not his dependent. She departed from the stereotype of the domestic woman. Her novels showed that women as well as men needed creative work to flourish. She rejected the idea of romantic love as the only legitimate basis for marriage: marriage was about mutual support, children, and surviving in life. Through her novels and stories she displayed her values of respect for the integrity of the person, particularly the integrity of the mind, and the equality of the sexes. Her view of romance as a man-woman relationship based on equality of respect and of opportunity developed despite her own painful experiences with the men in her life.

Although the characterisation in the early novels is not as fully developed as in her later fiction, Sayers always respected her characters and so created a coherent world for them to inhabit. The main characters develop through the novels, taking on a roundness and wholeness, and the subsidiary characters are never caricatures. Readers feel they know the Dowager Duchess, Mr. Murbles, Charles Parker, and Miss Climpson. Sayers is careful to manage the details of their lives across the novels.

4. Kenny, *Remarkable Case*, 192.

Sayers returned again and again to the question of "superfluous" women; a question which reflects both her society's assumption that the only worthwhile woman is a married woman, and the demographic fact that many women in her day were unable to marry because of the carnage of the First World War. The old maid, like Miss Twitterton in *Busman's Honeymoon*, was a figure of fun, mocked for being unattractive, for being sex starved and unbalanced, and for being useless and a drain on society. By way of contrast, in *Unnatural Death* Sayers introduces Miss Climpson, one of her best-loved characters.

Miss Climpson features in several Sayers novels and gives Sayers a chance to show the character of a woman who was deprived of a chance for what she would consider a normal life of husband and home, and of the education which would have made the most of her gifts of reasoning and retentive memory. "'A dear old friend of mine used to say that I should have made a very good lawyer,' said Miss Climpson, complacently, 'but of course, when I was young, girls didn't have the education or the *opportunities* they get nowadays'"[5] Miss Climpson makes the best of her life, learns from her experience in cheap boarding houses and vicarage tea parties to become a skilled judge of people, and a good detective. She is not of the same social class as Christie's Miss Marple, but both Miss Climpson and Miss Marple display a genius for detection through their nosiness . Miss Climpson is principled, charitable, thoroughly Christian and an attractive person. Miss Climpson runs The Cattery, a detective agency staffed by "women were of the class unkindly known as 'superfluous'" funded by Lord Peter.[6] Sayers describes one of the employees as thirty-eight and plain in a world which liked secretaries young and cheap.[7] The Cattery is Sayers' solution to the problems she observed with her aunts and recounted to Maurice Reckitt in a letter:

> I remember my father's sisters, brought up without education or training, thrown, at my grandfather's death, into a world that had no use for them. One, by my father's charity, was trained as a nurse; one, by wangling, was received into the only sisterhood that would take her at her age—an ill run community, but her only refuge; the third, the most attractive, lived peripatetically as a "companion" to various old cats, saving halfpence and cadging trifles, aimlessly

5. Sayers, *Strong Poison*, ch. 3.

6. Ibid., ch. 5.

7. Ibid., ch. 13.

doing what when done was of little value to God or man. From all such frustrate unhappiness, God keep us. Let us be able to write *"hoc feci"* on our tombstones, even if all we have done is to clean the 29 floors of the International Stores.[8]

Unpleasantness at the Bellona Club has four main women characters who personify various ways of coping with their opportunities. Old Lady Dormer, who had defied her family in youth to marry a manufacturer, lives with Ann Dorland, a young relative who is her companion. Dorland is not physically attractive, not particularly bright or talented, and lives on the fringes of the Bloomsbury crowd. Her friend and confidant, Marjorie Phelps is a successful sculptor who serves in several novels as a guide to the Bloomsbury set for Lord Peter. The fourth, Shelia Fentiman, is married to Lady Dorland's nephew, George. She suffers from his war-induced illness while working to support both of them. Shelia is constant and loves George without sentimentality; she is hurt by his sarcasm, but understands his frustration and his mental disturbance.

Lady Dormer is described as having had a happy marriage to her manufacturer and being generous to the family which disowned her, especially in the freedom she allows Ann, not expecting her to dance attendance and perform useless errands. Dorland eventually finds happiness as a wife. Sayers did not think that marriage was unimportant or always unsatisfying for women; what she deprecated was marriage as the sole vocation offered to any and every woman, without regard for the individual woman's desires and talents.

Sayers understood how men manipulated women seeking love, as she showed in her handling of Ann Dorland. Ann Dorland didn't belong in Bloomsbury: she had no specific talent in the creative arts that could give her the independence to survive the social shoals. She was unable to handle the "continual atmosphere of hectic passion."[9] Through Marjorie's descriptions of the Bloomsbury set, we see the free love of that set being as exploitative of women as the conventional marriage for financial security is. Ann had been jilted by a serial womaniser and then became involved with a doctor, who initially pursued her, but then, for his own reasons, dropped her. At their parting he told her she had imagined things, that she "had a mania about sex."[10] Wimsey wants to know what sort of mania, and is told,

8. Sayers, *Letters Vol. 2*, 320.
9. Sayers, *Unpleasantness*, ch. 10.
10. Ibid., ch. 20.

"Oh, the gibbering sort that hangs round church doors for curates . . . It's a lie. He did—he did—pretend to want me and all that. The beast! . . . I can't tell you the things he said . . . and I'd made such a fool of myself."[11] A similar scene occurs in *Busman's Honeymoon* where the middle-aged Miss Twitterton was courted by a younger man who had an eye on her savings. When their relationship ends, he uses the same sexual insults to repulse her.

Sayers was not blind to many women's domestic happiness, what she strongly condemned was the idea that a woman should find all her meaning and satisfaction in her love for her husband. This was idolatry and not true love. She showed this in her portrayals of characters drawn from all segments of the social system. The hinted at lesbian relationship between Mary Whitaker and Vera Finlayson in *Unnatural Death* is shown as destructive not because it is between two women, but because one of the women demands total devotion. This is as unhealthy as the demands men make for their wive's unquestioning devotion. It contrasts with the relationship of Eiluned Price and Sylvia Marriott in *Strong Poison*, two artists who may or may not be anything other than great friends, but whose friendship is a free relationship between equals.

Bloomsbury was important to Sayers in her own life, and she used it in several of her novels. It allowed her to people her novels with artists and to contrast their virtues and values with those of conventional society. She used an artists' colony in Scotland, where Sayers and Mac had vacationed, as a setting for *The Five Red Herrings*, a puzzle novel. She writes of people who are eccentric and often unconventional but who can really paint. This novel is the least satisfactory of her novels as fiction, because it is a pure puzzle book of railway timetables which Sayers wrote to test her skill. It is most interesting, however, as a picture of a community of artists, showing the satisfactions of creativity, the genuine virtues of the artists and their transgressions of respectability that come not from a desire to shock, but from their living according to a different set of values.

In the short story "The Unsolved Puzzle of the Man with No Face" the conflict between an artist's values and conventional standards leads directly to the crime. The artist can't support himself by his painting and must work in the studio of a publicity firm. The head of his department is a mean bully who wanted to the artist to paint a portrait of him. Wimsey expresses one of her core beliefs: "He thought that, by making the painter do it, he would get a good portrait at starvation price. But unhappily he'd forgotten that,

11. Ibid.

however much an artist will put up with in the ordinary way, he is bound to be sincere with his art. That's the one thing a genuine artist won't muck about with."[12]

In her novel, *The Documents in the Case* (1930), Sayers brings the themes of good work and equality in relationships together. She contrasts two marriages: a marriage of equals between John Munting and Elizabeth Drake that she later develops more fully in the Wimsey-Vane relationship, and a marriage that typifies the supposed ideal of the domesticity in the Harrisons. John Munting, observing the Harrison's marriage finds that "it was of his wife's personal life that he [Mr. Harrison] was jealous—her office, her interests, the friends she had made for herself—everything that had not come to her through him."[13] This expresses clearly, I think, Sayers' view of that no person should live only through a relationship: it makes the home a prison and sets the man in the place of God.

This novel's setting is Bayswater, a place of unimpeachable suburban morality. Lathom, the artist, says, "The suburbs are the only places left . . . where men and women will die and persecute for their beliefs. Artists believe in nothing . . . But the blessed people of the suburbs—they do believe in something. They believe in Respectability." [14] It is this quest for respectability that is the source of the murder. The contrast between the conventions of respectability and a genuine morality is a theme through all of Sayers' novels.

Sayers uses the Harrison's domestic help as an example of the tragedy of many of the superfluous women. In contrast to the well-balanced, useful Miss Climpson, Miss Milsom is shown as incompetent at both her housework and her crafts, and obsessed with sex and psychoanalysis, "She [Miss Milsom] consults these psycho-analytic quacks, who encourage her to attach an absurd importance to her whims and feelings . . . Besides, she is very lazy and untidy, and instead of putting her mind to the housework she litters the place with wool and bits of papers."[15]

Documents came out in the same year as Sayers produced *Strong Poison* in which Wimsey is the romantic as well as the detective hero, falling in love with Harriet Vane, a woman accused of poisoning her lover. Sayers claimed in the *Titles to Fame* article that she was planning to marry Wimsey

12. Sayers, *Lord Peter,* 236.

13. Sayers, *Documents,* Document 31.

14. Ibid.

15. Ibid., Document 24.

off and so be rid of him. When she found it impossible to marry her characters as they had developed in the novel, she expanded the boundaries of detective fiction, and through a series of books showed Peter and Harriet cautiously pursuing their relationship.

> I could not marry Peter off to the young woman he had (in the conventional Perseus manner) rescued from death and infamy, because I could find no form of words in which she could accept him without loss of self-respect. . . When I looked at the situation I saw that it was in every respect false and degrading; and the puppets had somehow got just so much flesh and blood in them that I could not force them to accept it without shocking myself.[16]

Ending the romance in the conventional way, that is in marriage, required six years of work, from 1930 to 1936, on the characters of Wimsey and Vane and on their relationship. In *Whose Body?* Wimsey appears to be a cross between Bertie Wooster and Sherlock Holmes with a legacy from the trenches of World War I: recurring nerve crises in the face of responsibility. Wimsey becomes a more developed character through the four novels dealing with the Wimsey-Vane relationship—*Strong Poison, Have His Carcase, Gaudy Night* and *Busman's Honeymoon.* Two novels which do not include Harriet, *Murder Must Advertise* and *The Nine Tailors*, are novels of transition where Wimsey develops from almost a caricature into a human being.

In an age in which gentlemen did not work, Sayers made work important to Wimsey through the full series. She introduces the question of work in *Whose Body?* She sets up a scene where Wimsey visits Parker and finds him reading a commentary on the Epistles of St. Paul. He asks Parker,

> "Do you like your job?"
> The detective considered the question, and replied,
> "Yes—yes, I do. I know it to be useful, and I am fitted to it. I do it quite well—not with inspiration, perhaps, but sufficiently well to take a pride in it. It is full of variety and it forces one to keep up to the mark and not get slack. And there's a future to it. Yes, I like it. Why?"[17]

She uses the conversation to establish Wimsey as someone who good at the job of detecting, but who has qualms about it. He detects but wants

16. Sayers, "Gaudy Night," 79.
17. Sayers, *Whose Body?* ch. 7.

to quit when someone is going to the gallows. Wimsey's essential dilemma, that by investigating murder he himself causes other deaths, sometimes the innocent, and often the murderer's death by execution, is handled with increasing subtlety over time.

The Wimsey-Vane romance is one of the great and enduring attractions of her detective fiction and a prime source for her ethics of marriage and work. She has managed to convey the possibility that a woman might be loved for herself not just for her appearance, or her skills in flirtation. Sayers is aiming at an ideal marriage: erotic delight and true friendship, with the wife not restricted to the confines of the home. Having the perfect man servant, Bunter, makes this easier, but her fiction does not gloss over the difficulties men had with economically independent women. Making the romance believable was hard work: Peter had been endowed by his creator with almost superhuman powers. In her novels preceding *Strong Poison*, Wimsey is shown to be an expert book collector, an accomplished musician, athletic, cultured, gourmet, wine connoisseur, and linguist. Harriet was fiercely independent and hurt by her previous relationship. What is truly unusual, I think, is Sayers' use of their integrity of mind and work as the means to establish the lovers on an equal footing capable of an ideal marriage.

Over the six years from 1930 until 1936 Sayers worked out the Peter/Harriet relationship, balancing the love interest, the demands of detective fiction, and her own convictions about intellectual integrity. She was searching for a way of putting Harriet on an equal footing with Peter. On one level *Strong Poison* is a conventional romance, girl rescued by hero. If the differences in wealth and class between Harriet and Peter were not quite that of a peasant girl and a king, they are significant. Harriet, instead of seeing this marriage as socially and economically advantageous and the proper step for any woman who has a duty to marry well, finds the wealth and social difference a hindrance. On another level *Strong Poison* is a morality tale about the double standard of conventional morality. Harriet Vane had lived with Philip Boyes without being married; that relationship was public and the public disapproval of it was made clear in the description of the trial and of Wimsey's friends and family's reaction to his interest in the case. Sayers shows how deeply Harriet had lost her self-respect when she answers Peter's offer of marriage with an offer to live with him instead, an offer he rejects. Harriet, privately and publicly shamed for betraying her own principles in pursuit of an ideal of love, despised herself so much that she could not begin to think of loving someone else.

Have His Carcase, which appeared in 1932, opens with Sayers' advice that the best cure for a bruised heart is not "repose upon a manly bosom", but "honest work, physical activity and the sudden acquisition of wealth."[18] In this we see the central theme of the entire Sayers' canon: the importance of creative, satisfying work in making a fully human life. Harriet finds her solace from the unpleasantness of her trial in her work and is experiencing some affluence from increased sales. Notoriety has its uses. Harriet discovers a murder victim as she is on a walking tour. Wimsey arrives to investigate along with her, and to her dismay, to protect her.

Sayers contrasts Harriet's and Peter's relationship with that of Mrs. Weldon, a middle-aged, wealthy widow, who was planning to marry a young dancer who worked at the seaside hotel. The relationship between Harriet and Peter works when they are intellectual partners working on the crime; it is the personal relationship, the "passionate politics" that Harriet finds impossible to get right. Together Peter and Harriet solve the mystery, one of Sayers' most complicated and torturous plots; but that brings no joy or resolution to their romantic relationship. Mrs Weldon's self-deception in her pathetic pursuit of love puts both Peter and Harriet off the idea of romance, at least temporarily.

The solution to the problem of the Peter-Harriet romance came through Sayers' invitation to propose the toast to the university at the Somerville Gaudy of 1934. Sayers, writing in *Titles to Fame* about *Gaudy Night,* makes clear how pivotal this experience was. Preparing for the speech made her ask "exactly what it was for which one had to thank a university education, and [I] came to the conclusion that it was, before everything, that habit of intellectual integrity which is at once the foundation and the result of scholarship."[19]

She had found her solution to three problems at once. First, her problem with her detective hero and his love: Harriet could stand equal to Peter on the intellectual platform. Secondly, she says: "By choosing a plot that should exhibit intellectual integrity as the one great permanent value in an emotionally unstable world I should be saying the thing that, in a confused way, I had been wanting to say all my life."[20] Finally, the theme of integrity of the work integrates the love story and the detective story in the novel.

18. Sayers, *Carcase*, ch. 1.
19. Sayers, "Gaudy Night," 82.
20. Ibid.

Gaudy Night (1935) is a mystery without a murder; it is the novel she discusses later in *The Mind of the Maker* when she is contrasting the problem-solving to the creative approach to life, the theme she develops fully in *The Mind of the Maker*. Writing the speech for the Gaudy, contemplating her own, at this time unsatisfactory, marriage, and writing a novel set in Oxford, she writes of integrity of the mind. This theme still resonates with novelists as in Ruth Dudley Edwards' novel *Matricide at St Martha's* where, after describing the actions of the head of the college, she has a character comment: "It's the same debate as in Dorothy Sayers's *Gaudy Night*—intellectual integrity as against the feelings of the flesh and blood people."[21] It is clear that Sayers is concerned with the integrity of all work. She as a scholar and a writer knew best the temptations of mental work. It would be a misreading, however, to limit her concern for integrity to only intellectual work. The theme of satisfying work was the central concern of her writing, whether religious or secular throughout her career. She notes this in *The Mind of the Maker* when she writes:

> I know it is no accident that *Gaudy Night,* coming towards the end of a long development in detective fiction, should be a manifestation of precisely the same theme as the play *The Zeal of Thy House,* which followed it and was the first in a series of creatures embodying a Christian theology. They are variations upon a hymn to a Master Maker: and now, after nearly twenty years, I can hear in *Whose Body?* the notes of that tune sounding unmistakably under the tripping melody of a very different descant: and further back still, hear it again, in a youthful set of stanzas in *Catholic Tales . . .* But the end is clearly there in the beginning.[22]

Gaudy Night is set in Oxford; that setting was integral to the plot for, as Catherine Kenney points out, "The setting is curiously appropriate to Harriet's consideration of marriage and its implications. A women's college is one of the few places where women are not perforce regarded simply in reference to men."[23] The main plot's romantic interest centres on the Peter-Harriet relationship. Through their honesty in confronting the conflicts between the demands of the personal and the demands of integrity in the work, Harriet is able to let go of her pride and accept that she is in love. Peter is also willing to ask forgiveness for his pushing his love on her; for

21. Edwards, *Matricide*, 167.

22. Sayers, *Mind of the Maker,* 207–8.

23. Kenney, *Remarkable*, 165.

his disregarding her feelings of inadequacy, for assuming that the love of a good man will solve all problems.

Peter's apology is only possible from a man who has moved well beyond the conventions of romance. In his courtship of Harriet up until this point, he has scrupulously observed the dictates of courtly love: he does not use his knowledge as a man of the world to pursue Harriet. He serves her, accepting the most daunting treatment from her but staying constant in his love. He continues to court her in this tradition: they sit up kissing in the punt, but the consummation of their physical relationship is reserved for their marriage.

As with all of Sayers' novels, the secondary characters are as illuminating and fully drawn as the protagonists. They advance both the theme and the plot of the book. During her residence in the college, we, through Harriet's eyes, become acquainted with various students including Miss Cattermole. Miss Cattermole wants to be loved and, of course, married. She had wanted to study cookery, but, "'My mother's one of those people who work to get things open to women—you know—professions and things. And my father's a lecturer in a small provincial University. And they've made a lot of sacrifices and things.' . . . Harriet thought Miss Cattermole was probably the sacrificial victim."[24]

The dons of the Senior Common Room, the "elderly virgins" as the Dean describes them, have made the other choice available to a woman, a career and no love or passion.

Annie, the criminal, is one of the college servants. In the book she is shown as enthusiastic when Harriet inquires after her children, and recommends that Harriet get married herself saying, "But it seems to me a dreadful thing to see all these unmarried ladies living together. It isn't natural, is it?"[25] Annie thinks the library a waste, "I can't see what girls want with books. Books won't teach them to be good wives."[26] When it appears that Annie will have to remove her children from their current carer because of the husband's possibly criminal behaviour, she says, "I'm the last person to wish to put difficulties into the way of a respectable married woman . . . and naturally she's right to stick by her husband. . . He's her husband and she has to take his part, I quite see that."[27]

---

24. Sayers, *Gaudy Night*, ch. 8.

25. Ibid., ch. 5.

26. Ibid.

27. Ibid., ch. 8.

At the dénouement, when Annie is accused of causing the disturbances in the college, she doesn't deny it but defends herself as revenging the ill treatment academia had meted out to her husband: "couldn't you leave my man alone? He told a lie about somebody else who was dead and dust hundreds of years ago. Nobody was the worse for that. Was a dirty bit of paper more important than all our lives and happiness?"[28] Annie, like Mr. Harrison, shows the idolatry and perversion of all virtues that the ideology of the good wife and mother can produce.

Gaudy Night maintains that respect for persons must include respect for the person's work. Sayers makes this point very early in the book in a conversation between Harriet Vane and one of the dons, Miss Barton. Miss Barton wonders that after her terrible experience of being accused of murder, Miss Vane would continue to write mysteries. Harriet's answer is straightforward, yes, proper feeling might dictate that any other kind of work might be preferable, but "I should scrub floors very badly, and I write detective stories rather well. I don't see why proper feeling should prevent me from doing my proper job."[29]

The place of productive work in the courtship is a central theme of the novel. Harriet, although physically attracted to Peter, can hold him at arm's length. It is when Peter takes her work seriously that she can believe that he wants a relationship of equals. He tells her she hasn't yet written the book she is capable of, and recommends that she make her characters three-dimensional. When she objects that it would hurt like hell, he replies, "What does it matter if it makes a good book."[30]

The novel ends with Peter and Harriet retrieving their relationship, not by ignoring the past but redeeming it. Harriet had accepted the condemnation that the double standard of sexual morality allotted her. She could rise above it when Peter recognises her work as having integrity. This may strike many readers as unrealistic; but it is a common justification for not condemning male public figures for their private lives, however messy. This text is the challenge to the orthodoxy of heterosexuality: that men have lives and women live only for love; that women can be defined only by a relationship with a man. *Gaudy Night* necessarily finishes at the engagement. *Busman's Honeymoon* takes the relationship to the next stage and shows that no marriage is automatically "happily ever after."

28. Ibid., ch. 22.
29. Ibid., ch. 2.
30. Ibid., ch. 14.

The Wimsey-Vane romance presents not a return to a medieval idea of marriage or of courtly love, but uses both of those conceptions of love and marriage to create an alternative to the ideology of romantic love and the domestic woman. Marriage is both more pedestrian, and more exalted. It is a partnership of equals, an exchange of felicity and one of the goods in a full human life, but by no means the only good, or the only relationship of importance to men or to women. She has shown the double standard of sexual morality as being overcome by a respect for the woman's work. She has also shown how deeply the stereotypes of gender and expected behaviour run: both Peter and Harriet lapse into conventional words and expectations. They, however, are old enough, and wise enough to question what they are doing, and reject the stereotypes.

In between writing the novels of the Wimsey-Vane romance, Sayers produced two detective novels which didn't involve the romance. *The Nine Tailors* was a work of love centered on a great Fenland church, which took much longer to write than Sayers' had anticipated. She paid the bills with *Murder Must Advertise,* a mystery set in the world of advertising, which she knew from her work at Bensons. It describes the world of work in the office with an eye that observes and dissects the community that forms in any workplace and it marks the first appearance of the three-part analogy of creative mind which she goes on to write in the epilogue to *The Zeal of Thy House,* and to examine in relation to the doctrine of the Trinity in *The Mind of the Maker.*

She later described the plot as unsuccessful; she had two artificial worlds, the Bright Young Things, and advertising. Wimsey appears in disguise in both worlds. Her thinly disguised account of life in an ad agency in *Murder Must Advertise* showed a firm that treated employees with respect, although paternalistically as you would expect for that era. The victim in that mystery was not liked because he did not hold up the standard of honesty that was expected. Wimsey investigating the death inquires why Dean wasn't liked and is told, "Why, because he didn't play fair. He was always snooping round other people's rooms, picking up their ideas and showing them up as his own."[31]

Her description of the process of creating a big advertising campaign for a cigarette called Whifflets, produced three incidents in the narrative which correspond to the three parts of her analogy for the Trinity that

31. Sayers, *Murder Must Advertise,* ch. 3.

developed in her writing over the next years. First we have the description of what she will later call the IDEA, an analogy for the Father:

> It is not to be supposed that the great Whiffle-Way in all its comprehensive perfection, sprang fully formed from Mr. Bredon's brain when Mr. Armstrong uttered the words, Family Appeal. All that then happened was a mental association with the phrase Family Hotel, coupled with a faint consciousness of inner illumination. He replied humbly, "Yes, I see; I'll try to work out something," gathered up some sheets of paper on which Mr. Armstrong had scribbled a few illegible notes and a thing that looked like a hedgehog, and made his way out. He had taken six steps down the passage when the idiotic slogan: "If that's what you want, you can Whiffle for it," took possession of his brain; two steps further on, this repellent sentence had recast itself as: "All you Want by Whiffling," and on the threshold of his own room, the first practical possibility of Whiffledom struck him like a sledgehammer.[32]

The IDEA for Sayers is the glimpse of the whole, without beginning or end. But to work any Idea out, either as a book, a painting or an advertising campaign requires activity. She describes the activity which she later calls ENERGY, an analogy for the Son:

> "I like this scheme, Mr. Bredon," said Mr Pym, tapping his finger on the drafts submitted to him. "It has Breadth. It has Vision. More than anything else, Advertising needs Vision and Breadth. That is what determines Appeal. In my opinion, this scheme of yours has Appeal. It is going to be expensive, of course, and needs some working out. For instance, if all these vouchers were cashed in at once, it would send up the cost per packet to a figure that the profits could not possibly cover. But I think that can be got over."
> "They won't all be cashed in at once," said Mr. Armstrong.
> The two directors plunged into a maze of facts and figures.[33]

Here is the central dilemma of creativity: getting the idea embodied in time and space, in a fallen world. The analogy isn't yet complete.

When the work is done and the IDEA is embodied in the activity or ENERGY, it creates a reaction in the creator and anyone else who sees it. Sayers calls this the POWER, the response, an analogy for the Holy Spirit. At the end of the novel Sayers pictures Wimsey is standing on the street:

32. Ibid., ch. 15.
33. Ibid., ch. 16.

A bus passed bearing a long ribbon display upon its side:
WHIFFLE YOUR WAY ROUND BRITAIN!
The great campaign had begun. He contemplated his work with a kind of amazement. With a few idle words on a sheet of paper he had touched the lives of millions.[34]

In *Murder Must Advertise*, the three parts of creative mind are present implicitly. In her work as a playwright, she experiences creation in a new way, in a process with living, intelligent actors.

Her writing about the theater indicates that it was this experience which forged the final link between her experience as a writer and the Christian theology of the Trinity. The analogy between artistic creation and the Trinity, implicit in *Murder Must Advertise*, became explicit in the practical life of the theater. In "The Christian Faith and the Theater" she wrote: "But if he [the playwright] is humble and prepared to take a very realistic view of his own deficiencies he does, nevertheless, undergo the tremendous and almost terrifying experience of seeing his own word made flesh."[35] She went on to compare the typescript of a play to a prophecy of creation; and wrote of the "miracle":

> But when the rehearsal begins, then the miracle begins. The maker of the play sees his word animating, and as it were, making for itself a body out of living flesh and blood. Not only that, but a corporate or common body inhabited by wills independent of his own, which, yet, by the power of that word which is himself, are subdued and responsive to his will, conforming all that they are to his word dwelling and acting within them rendering him back to himself a kind of living mirror, so that his own thought is at once within himself and also manifest outside him incarnate in a fully-conscious, fully self-willed and partly independent creative form.
>
> Speaking only for myself, I can only say that this miracle never fails to move me. It is experienced at its freshest and most astonishing at the first rehearsal of each new play. I think that if I were to write a hundred new plays, it would never lose its power to startle . . . me.[36]

In *The Mind of the Maker* she claims writing for the stage much more interesting to the author than writing for publication.

---

34. Ibid., ch. 21.
35. Sayers, "Christian Faith," 8.
36. Ibid., 9–10.

> To hear an intelligent and sympathetic actor infusing one's own lines with his creative individuality is one of the most profound satisfactions that any imaginative writer can enjoy; more—there is an intimately moving delight in watching the actor's mind at work to deal rightly with a difficult interpretation . . . Within the limits of this human experience, the playwright has achieved that complex end of man's desire—the creation of a living thing with a mind and will of its own."[37]

Collaborating with Muriel St Clair Byrne on *Busman's Honeymoon*, the culmination of the Wimsey-Vane relationship, gave her these experiences. Fulfilling the commission for the Canterbury festival plays allowed her to show in the play the connection between her ideas on creativity and integrity of the work and Christian dogma. The BBC commissions allowed her to tackle the Gospels directly, and use her gifts to show the message.

That this new phase in her career should give rise to the Trinitarian analogy of *The Mind of the Maker* is no coincidence given the unique nature of collaboration and response which writer, actors, musicians, technicians, audience and critics bring to the field. As a result, the plays themselves provide a further opportunity for the presentation of her theory about creative mind.

The dogmas of the Incarnation and the Trinity give us a framework within which to understand humans as bearing the image of God. The Trinity and the Incarnation are as inseparable for Sayers as for Athanasius. Because God became man, matter is sacramental. Humans are created with the capacity to create, and the capacity to know God. Sayers concentrated on the analogy with the capacity to create, within an unstated acceptance that the purpose of life was to be in right relationship with the Creator. With that understanding of the human, she drew her ethic with its central concern of the integrity of work. An important corollary of these doctrines is the equality of men and women. Sayers' plays, *Busman's Honeymoon* and *Love All* are secular dramas which directly deal with the question of men and women and their work.

Busman's Honeymoon opened on 16 December 1936 in London at the Comedy Theater. It is typical of Sayers that she insisted that the play adhere to the fair play rules of detective fiction: no clue could be visible to the detective that wasn't visible to the audience. The discipline of the theater made this an interesting project, since misdirection needed to be handled

37. Sayers, *Mind*, 63.

in a different way and for a much longer time than is necessary in a novel where the reader quickly turns the page to find out what happened next.

The play takes up the Wimsey-Vane relationship at the honeymoon. Peter and Harriet have decided to honeymoon in a country house, necessary so that there is no electricity, only lamps. Their first night is uncomfortable, none of the arrangements the landlord promised have been made. They cope, with the miracle working Bunter. Naturally, they cannot have a peaceful time, but discover a body on their premises.

Busman's Honeymoon continued the theme of the integrity of the work from *Gaudy Night*. In the quarrel scene, Harriet wants to escape from the mess of the investigation. Peter tells her his hands are hangman's hands, but then relents and offers to give up the investigation if it upsets her. Harriet rejects his offer. When the leading actors in the play were given this scene, they thought it had no relationship to life. The play opened in the midst of the abdication crisis; an example of the conflict between love understood as a virtue among the other virtues of prudence, temperance and justice, and love as the romantic ideal. The audience knew what Sayers meant if her actors did not: "Miss Byrne, prowling about the upper circle at the moment when Harriet says, "What kind of life would we have if I knew you had become less than yourself by marrying me?" was gratified to catch the syllables "Mrs. Simpson!" hissed fiercely by a woman to her neighbour.[38]

Through the play Peter and Harriet fall into the trap of conventional stereotypes of husband and wife. They work through these, and recognise that this was bound to happen, and that they can cope with it. After Peter solves the mystery, though, we see exactly what solidarity in guilt means. His action is going to result in another person's death. In answer to his desire not to have meddled Harriet points out that innocent lives were at risk, someone could have been arrested who had not been responsible for the murder. She also reminds him that if he hadn't meddled six years ago, she would have been executed. Out of all that evil, the good of their marriage comes. There is the Christian structure of human life that Sayers saw clearly and expressed through her novels. The fault in man, God's creation, means that our evil can never be totally bad, and our good always tinged with some evil. Our work is to redeem this world: to take the situation we are given and make something new; even as we recognise that that new thing will have its flaws.

38. Sayers, *Letters Vol. 1*, 414.

When the hour of the execution strikes, he is on his knees, cradled by Harriet as he begins to weep. Here is the total oversetting of the gender stereotypes of romantic love. The man is weak and relies on the woman; weakness, though, is the central paradox of the Christian faith: it is when we are weak and are seemingly crushed by evil that good can overcome. We can find personal healing, and begin to heal the violence evil creates. Sayers' ideal marriage recognises the truth of the human condition, its fallen nature, solidarity in guilt and its need to conquer pride. Men and women equally suffer the effects of the fall. Men and women equally can love in a way that brings good from evil.

Gaudy Night and *Busman's Honeymoon* are the idealization of equality in marriage; *Love All* is a light comedy that conveys the same message, both men and women need meaningful work. *Love All* is a portrayal of marriages as experienced by many women who fulfil society's expectations and become good wives and mothers. To the world around them they become not only an asexual being but almost a non-being. The good wife is abandoned by her husband. Instead of repining while the affair was beginning she wrote a play which became successful. Sayers contrived the plot so that the wronged wife forgets to divorce her erring husband in the pressure of her new career as the playwright, Janet Reed. The mistress, Lydia, is an actress who misses her proper work, and comes to London to ask for a role in Janet Reed's new play, not knowing Janet Reed is the wronged wife. Godfrey, the erring husband, cannot understand why these women want to have jobs, rather than stay at home being his inspiration. He ends up abandoned by wife, mistress and secretary. In the play, the wife says, "It's grand to be liked for what one can do." She tells her husband that she has found romance in finding herself, rather than trying to find it in other people.[39]

In between writing the two romantic plays, Sayers was working on the Canterbury Festival play, based on the Latin chronicle by Gervase the Monk which detailed the rebuilding of the Cathedral after the disastrous fire of 1174. The theme allowed her to express her interest in integrity in work which formed the theme of *Gaudy Night*, in the new medium she loved, the theater.

The Zeal of Thy House intertwines the themes of Incarnation, the Trinity and the ethic of work: the three strands which are virtually inseparable in all of her writing about work. *Gaudy Night* had shown the disruption to personal lives that integrity in work could cause, and the devastation that

39. Sayers, *Love All*, 175.

follows from allowing the personal to override the internal demands of the practice of the work, in that case, intellectual inquiry. In this play, through the character of William of Sens the architect, but also in the characters of the monks and manual workers she returns to this conflict of the personal and the requirements of the work, and then examines this conflict in the light of her understanding of the great drama of Christian salvation.

The theme of integrity in work occurs early in the play. In a conversation between the Prior and Theodatus, the Sacristan, the latter claims a preference for a worse built church and a virtuous builder while the Prior calls to witness the example of the Church built on Peter, the liar and coward, but also the rock and common man, rather than on John who was all gold. The Prior leaves the judgement to God: "Do your own work, while yet the daylight lasts. Look that it be well done; look not beyond it."[40]

The main character is William of Sens, the master craftsman chosen to rebuild the choir. His morals are conventionally bad: he is having an affair with Lady Ursula, and cooking the books to get the materials he needs. However, he is a great workman; he has vision and inspires his craftsmen. Sayers has four angels on stage throughout the play: Michael, Gabriel, Raphael and Cassiel. The angels give background to the action, focus the audience on the theological issues, provide light relief, and visually display the irony of our lives: that all unaware, we live under the gaze of God and his angels. The angels tell us of William's sins, but to his credit they count the building he has done, which is straight and true. Raphael says, "Behold, he prayeth; not with lips alone,/But with the hand and the cunning brain"[41]

William is confident in his work, and it is his besetting sin, pride.

> And lastly, since all Heaven was not enough
> To share that triumph, He made His masterpiece,
> Man, that like God can call beauty from dust,
> Order from chaos, and create new worlds
> To praise their maker. Oh, but in making man
> God over-reached Himself and gave away
> His Godhead. He must now depend on man
> For what man's brain, creative and divine
> Can give Him. Man stands equal with Him now,
> Partner and rival.[42]

---

40. Sayers, *Four Sacred Plays,* 61.

41. Ibid., 38.

42. Ibid., 68.

Here an analogy between creator, human and divine, is distorted by a desire to emulate the power of God. When humans' passion for creativity causes them to forget they are creatures, they fall into pride. William's pride in his work causes him to trust his safety to a monk scandalized by his affair with Lady Ursula and a worker who was watching her rather than the rope he was to inspect. The near-fatal accident that follows prevents William from completing his work of art. His idea is not fully realised in effect (at least, not by him) because he sees nothing divine in the work.

The sin of pride is tempered by the sympathetic response of William's associates. It is as if the suppression of his skills as an artist is a penalty in excess of his sin. Gervase exclaims, "Part from his work? Oh no! It would be more bitter to him than death."[43] And then, in a fascinating vignette, William himself describes in microcosm the effect of what he has now done to himself:

> . . .A year ago
> An idle mason let the chisel slip
> Spoiling the saint he carved. I chid him for it,
> Then took the tool and in that careless stroke
> Saw a new vision, and so wrought it out
> Into a hippogriff. But yet the mason
> Was not the less to blame. So works with us
> The cunning craftsman, God.[44]

Here, the error is redeemed by the vision of a second artist (a second Adam?) but, unlike the activity of God, the finished work is not consistent with the original idea.

Sayers knew that ordinary people had severe difficulties with the idea of judgment even though they were conscious of sin. Atonement, which is inseparable from any understanding of the dual nature of Christ, was the crux of her religious plays. She shows Michael the archangel cutting the rope, yet she has each of the people take responsibility for their part of the tragedy. Ursula is remorseful for coming to the building and distracting the workman. Simon the workman is penitent for his neglect. Only the scandalized monk tries to justify himself, but the Prior reprimands him, "This is thy sin: thou hast betrayed the work; thou hast betrayed the Church; thou hast betrayed Christ in the person of his fellow man."[45]

43. Ibid., 79.
44. Ibid., 91.
45. Ibid., 75.

William confesses his sins to the Prior. He can see his affair with the Lady Ursula and his financial trickery as sin but is blind to his pride. The archangel Michael confronts him and tells him his sin is where his heart is, in his work. William denies this, and claims that Christ cannot take his work from him. Michael tells him of Christ's death and resurrection, "For lo! God died—and still His work goes on."[46]

In the end, William understands and is saved:

> . . . Thou that didst make the world
> And wilt not let one thing that Thou hast made,
> No, not one sparrow, perish without Thy Will
> (Since what we make, we love)—for that love's sake
> Smite only me and spare my handiwork. . .
> Let me lie deep in hell,
> Death gnaw upon me, purge my bones with fire,
> But let my work, all that was good in me,
> All that was God, stand up and live and grow.[47]

Sayers' sense of a "complete picture" under which the artist exercises his or her skill meant that she understood the artist telling a truth, a reflection of a reality beyond the work of the individual. The process of cooperation between the audience which was to respond creatively to the work of art, and the artists and craftsmen who were contributing their disparate skills to a single uniform idea is a living model of the Trinity. The Trinity is essentially relational. Sayers herself had lived an analogy to this relationality in the theater where actors, musicians and producers were ineffectual without costume designers, lighting technicians, and stagehands. This necessary cooperation for the achievement of the end was true of the rebuilding of the Canterbury Quire as William suggests:

> All these [i.e., carpenter, workmaster, smith, potter] trust to their hands
> and every one is wise in his work.
> Without these cannot a city be inhabited, and they shall not dwell
> where they will nor go up and down;
> They shall not be sought for in public council, nor sit high in the
> congregation;
> But they will maintain the state of the world, and all their desire is in
> the work of their craft.[48]

46. Ibid., 98.
47. Ibid., 99.
48. Ibid., 34–35.

Sayers will develop this theory in her wartime writing where she makes a general call for workers to understand the value of the work they are called to do and to understand their contribution to the greater picture. This theme of a person's one skill or expertise contributing to the whole is developed in a conversation between Gervase and William in which the former admits, "I must be content to be the man with only one talent, and make it go as far as I can." William responds, "If everyone would make good use of his own talent and let others do the same, the world would move faster."[49] Sayers called for responsibility—every one must grapple with evil and transform it into good. The pattern of the crucifixion and resurrection cannot be avoided by anyone. All must be responsible for their actions which will never be fully good, or totally evil. The past cannot be changed but it can be redeemed.

The play culminates in the speech of the Archangel Michael which articulates in embryo the theory of Sayers which provides the basis for her analogy between the doctrine of the Trinity and the creative writer's trinity of idea, energy, and power. The speech was cut from the first performance of this play at Canterbury in 1937 by Harcourt Williams, the producer who played William. He felt it was anti-climax after the dramatic exit of William. Sayers admired Williams and, if he thought that the dramatic structure of the piece was better served without the speech, Sayers accepted his opinion. It is perhaps ironic that a speech which articulated the concept of the unity of an artist's vision from idea through to effect was cut on the advice of a different artist. The play was published with the speech intact.

Sayers' imaginative writing from the first embodied her faith in the Incarnation and the Trinity. In the detective novels she critiques the gender stereotypes of her day, and shows what a relationship of true equality might look like. In her religious plays, she could be more explicit about the dogma that was the framework for the drama. Sayers' analogy for the Trinity to the artist's experience of creation is central to her conception of good work. It appears in the description of Lord Peter working on an advertising campaign. In *Zeal* she was able to put it into Christian language and relate it to the daily lives of Christians. This is the key truth she wished to communicate through her articles and speeches during the war years, which is the subject of the next chapter.

49. Ibid., 39.

3

Sayers' Wartime Writing

SAYERS' RELIGIOUS WRITING WAS commissioned. She was not seeking to become a public advocate of Christianity, nor was she bombarding editors with her theological writing. She became a public apologist for Christianity through her religious plays, and used her position responsibly. Sayers' importance as a thinker and writer on social ethics during the war years is underappreciated. It may seem as if she were simply a celebrity that the Church of England used for her name recognition. I maintain that William Temple, as Archbishop of York and then Archbishop of Canterbury, recognized Sayers' gifts as a lay theologian and the quality and depth of her thought.

To understand Sayers' role in the public discussion of social ethics, and particularly of the challenges of constructing a post-war world that would be more just, I will discuss the tradition of Anglican social ethics, and especially William Temple, who is such an important figure in social ethics. Anglican social ethics had diverse streams of thought united by the Anglican self-understanding of theology as grounded in Scripture, tradition and reason. Sayers' work and her ideas about doctrine and translation, and especially her conception of the sacramentality of creation place her in the natural law stream of Anglican Social Ethics. As such she could take part in the ecumenical conversation on social ethics which marked this period. Catholics, Anglicans and Free Church adherents had a robust discussion of how to create a better world, having learned from the aftermath of World War I that peace has to be won. Sayers was at the heart of this.

She wrote to alert people to the dangers of saying "No more war," to bolster morale, to encourage personal responsibility, and to help make people think about the post-war world. Her speeches were often issued as pamphlets, and many of them were later collected in two works, *Creed or Chaos* (1947) and *Unpopular Opinions* (1946). Her speeches were reported in the religious as well as in the secular press and the reports show the continuation of her main themes of personal responsibility based on a sacramental understanding of the world and the importance of human work. The seemingly diverse output is unified in being structured on the Christian creeds, the framework for her dramas, which she translates into current speech in her expository writings. This work, produced in wartime when people demanded answers to the great questions, Why is there evil? Why are we here? What is man? has much to teach us today when a global economic crisis has left many distrusting the institutions of state and church, and wondering how to make a good human life.

She identified her method as translating one jargon into another which requires that the translator understand both jargons. Sayers' translation partners—Scholastic philosophy into common speech in mid-20th century England, Biblical speech into scholastic philosophy —show her sensitivity to the qualities a good translator needs: knowing not only the words and idioms, but also the history and the cultural underpinnings which give the language its shape and present form.

In the 1937 letter to Fr. Kelly she discussed the point of translation and the equally important point of intellectual rather than emotional faith; what she worried about was not lay people thinking about theology, but their having "a lack of practice in handling technical terms."[1] After her first articles on Christian doctrine appeared in *The Sunday Times* in 1938, she was inundated with invitations to speak on religious topics, and was generally willing to do so in one of two ways, either translating the creeds into modern idiom, or telling the churchmen exactly what kind of wildly mistaken ideas the majority of people had about Christianity.[2] She knew why she was called upon so often. In a letter to John, later Cardinal, Heenan she wrote: "I think one of the troubles is that so few parsons are really trained

1. Sayers, *Letters Vol. 2*, 51–52.
2. Ibid., 116.

to the use of words. They use the standard technical phrases without quite realising how they sound to the ordinary reader or listener." [3]

The key point in most of her presentations that "the heathen" had no idea about what Christianity actually taught: "The trouble is that, in nine cases out of ten, he has never been offered the dogma. What he has been offered is a set of technical theological terms which nobody has taken the trouble to translate into language relevant to ordinary life . . . nine out of ten of my heretics are exceedingly surprised to discover that the Creeds contain any statements that bear a practical and comprehensible meaning."[4]

The creeds were her touchstone, only then could she be sure that she wasn't leading people into apostasy. She explained to Bishop Talbot, this time in connection with the series of talks they were giving on the BBC, that she would be explaining rather than exhorting people to belief. Sayers thought Bishop Talbot was an example of how churchmen talk without considering the audience and their understanding, "I am reduced to complete pulp by Bishop Talbot, who says that in FOUR talks devoted to *Why we want a God to believe in*, it has not occurred to him to explain what is meant by the word 'Sin'!!!!" [5]

She was fitted for this work of translation, and was aware of the pitfalls. In a letter to the Rev. T. Wigley she remarked that it is impractical to only use modern idiom when dealing with theology for two reasons:

1. The mere fact that we have to deal with the Bible obliges us to make use of the theological ideas and expressions in which it abounds. . . . Many, indeed of the most crude and erroneous ideas about doctrine (especially as regards redemption) are directly derived from the reading of the Bible without sufficient knowledge of its theological and historical backgrounds.

2. The older theological words and expressions formed a real technical vocabulary, and it is at least possible to discover and say what they meant to the theologians who used them.[6]

Her dislike of personal questions and her emphasis on personal responsibility contributed to her choice of method. She was prepared to explain, but wanted people to think for themselves and make up their own

---

3. Ibid., 179–80.

4. Sayers, *Creed*, 33–35.

5. Sayers, *Letters Vol. 2*, 260.

6. Ibid., 288.

minds. Taking responsibility for thinking, not being led by the crowd or propaganda was the theme of *Begin Here* and a secondary theme in all her essays on work. This concern for intellect is reflected in her concern for logic and clear thinking. She repeatedly told people that they are free to believe or disbelieve Christianity. What she wanted to do is make sure that they understand exactly what it is they are accepting or rejecting. And she was dissatisfied with the general level of reading in a culture which boasted of almost 100 per cent literacy.

The conflict of assumptions within British life was becoming plainer throughout the 1920s and 1930s. Communism offered an alternative tradition to Christianity, Fascism tried to do the same. A large proportion of the literate fell into the category Sayers names Jesuanists: they accepted Jesus as a great moral teacher but not as the Son of God. Some had a vague idea of a deity "out there" though many were materialists and determinists. Sayers told churchmen that the people's problems of belief arose from their fundamental misunderstanding and distortion of what Christianity was and what it taught. Sayers believed Christianity's dogma and the consequent ethics could answer the challenges of science, psychology, and the social dislocation in her culture.

Sayers began her career as a public Christian with interviews to publicize *The Zeal of Thy House*, when it moved to the West End in 1938. Sayers, experienced in the value of advertising, gave interviews which emphasized Christian dogma as the framework for the play. In an age when the Christianity was perceived as a great moral system, burdened with an irrelevant dogma that was the relic of earlier, credulous ages, her position attracted great attention. She was asked to write an article for the *Sunday Times* for Passion Sunday clarifying what she meant. She obliged with "The Greatest Drama Ever Staged is the Official Creed of Christendom" in which she attempts to answer the question "What does the Church think of Christ?" (quoted above) in language which is clear and contemporary and most definitely not the normal vocabulary of Christianity as the public was accustomed to it.

The response to her article was so positive that the editor commissioned another for Easter Sunday, "The Triumph of Easter." She links Easter and the question of the time, "Why doesn't God smite this dictator dead?" Her answer is characteristically robust and insightful: "Why, madam, did He not strike you dumb and imbecile before you uttered that baseless and unkind slander the day before yesterday? Or me, before I behaved which such cruel lack of consideration to that well-meaning friend? And why, sir, did He not cause your hand to rot off at the wrist before you signed your name to that dirty little bit of financial trickery?"[7]

She suggests, however, that this is not the most significant or interesting question. The real question is, "Why should God, if there is a God, create anything, at any time, of any kind at all?"[8] The answer, Sayers suggests (three years before she wrote *The Mind of the Maker*) might be given by the creative artist. The obstacle to this search for an answer is the fact that the artist is less likely to wish to provide such an answer since he or she may regard creative activity as its own sufficient justification. Nevertheless, Sayers pursues the possibility and begins to use the language which lies at the root of her argument in *Mind*.

> But we may all, perhaps, allow that it is easier to believe the universe to have come into existence for some reason than for no reason at all. The Church asserts that there is a Mind which made the universe, that He made it because He is the sort of Mind that takes pleasure in creation, and that if we want to know what the Mind of the Creator is, we must look at Christ. In Him, we shall discover a Mind that loved His own creation so completely that He became part of it, suffered with and for it, and made it a sharer in His own glory and a fellow-worker with Himself in the working out of His own design for it.[9]

The words, "Mind," "Creator," "fellow-worker" and "design" are words for which Sayers had great affinity. That they took the Church in the right direction for an answer to the ultimate question was meat and drink to the creative artist who provided a unique and empirical analogy to the Church's most distracting of dogmas: the doctrine of the Holy Trinity.

In the same month, April 1938, she published "The Dogma is the Drama" in *St Martin's Review*. In it she explained that discussions with the actors in her Canterbury play, *The Zeal of Thy House*, showed her how ignorant the general populace was about the meaning of Christianity. Sayers listed reactions to *Zeal* which included disbelief on the part of some "that the Eternal Word was supposed to be associated in any way with the work of Creation" and "that the doctrine of the Trinity could be considered to

---

7. Sayers, *Creed*, 8.

8. Ibid., 8.

9. Ibid., 9–10.

have any relation to fact or any bearing on psychological truth."[10] She presents an examination paper with the answers that might be given by most members of the populace and highlights their lack of knowledge about what the Church teaches: "Q: What is the doctrine of the Trinity? A.: The Father incomprehensible, the Son incomprehensible and the whole thing incomprehensible. Something put in by theologians to make it more difficult—nothing to do with daily life or ethics."[11]

The Trinity was not the only misunderstood doctrine; the theology of the atonement presents real difficulties:

> Q. What is meant by the Atonement?
>
> A. God wanted to damn everybody, but His vindictive sadism was sated by the crucifixion of His own Son, who was quite innocent, and, therefore, a particularly attractive victim. He now only damns people who don't follow Christ or who never heard of Him.[12]

In all of these articles she saw herself not as being original but as using her skill as a craftsman in words to make clear the dogma of the Church. This dogma was an explanation of the universe that the public was free to accept or reject; her job was to make sure they understood exactly what they were usually rejecting without thought. The *Times* articles and the BBC broadcast of her nativity play in 1938 made Sayers known as a Christian writer to a wider and more diverse audience than those who would attend a Canterbury Festival play. Sayers became part of public Christianity and did not refuse the responsibilities which followed.

She was invited to speak at a women's conference and responded with the essay which proposed "Are Women Human?" as the true question for society. The essay goes on to dissect stereotyping, good and bad. The revolutionary position, Sayers maintains, is that women are ordinary human beings. So, to answer "what jobs, if any, are women's jobs" one must ask what the qualifications are necessary for the job and allow anyone, male or female who has those qualifications to do the job. She had tackled the same question in a different genre in the play *Love All*. This pattern, of approaching an issue using several genres of writing, is repeated through the next years.

10. Ibid., 21.
11. Ibid., 22.
12. Ibid., 22–23.

In April 1939, the *Sunday Times* commissioned another article; Sayers responded with "The Food for the Full Grown" later published as "Strong Meat"[13] She argues that Christianity is a religion for adult minds and interprets Jesus' call to his followers to enter the kingdom of heaven as little children as an encouragement to start each day with a keen enthusiasm and zest for life as one might have known at the age of five. She dismisses the assumption that time is evil in itself and that it brings nothing but deterioration. Again, she summons the artist to the aid of her argument: "His opinion would have been of great interest, since he might have spoken with authority of the soul's development in Time, of the vigorous grappling with evil that transforms it into good, of the dark night of the soul that precedes crucifixion and issues in resurrection."[14]

The artist will be able to do this because he or she may be assumed to have achieved some measure of "triumphant fulfilment." Much of her description of the artist's authority is reminiscent of the second person of the creative writer's trinity—the energy, to which belongs everything that can be included under the word "passion."

When the war began Sayers used her position to first, ask that the churches be kept open during the war even if the theatres had to close, and second, to ask the public "What Do We believe?"[15] This article in *The Sunday Times* starts with a typically vivid scene:

> cut off from mental distractions by restrictions and blackouts, and cowering in a cellar with a gas-mask under threat of imminent death, comes in the stronger fear and sits down beside us.
>
> "What," he demands, rather disagreeably, "do you make of all this? Is there indeed anything you value more than life, or are you making a virtue of necessity? What do you believe? Is your faith a comfort to you under the present circumstances?"[16]

She then examines the clauses of the Christian creed and highlights the creative mind as the image of God we bear: "we assert further that the will and power to make is an absolute value, the ultimate good-in-itself, self-justified, and self-explanatory."[17] The article functions as a short summary of the ideas she will develop in *The Mind of the Maker*.

13. Ibid., 14–19.
14. Ibid., 17–18.
15. Sayers, *Unpopular Opinions*, 17
16. Ibid.
17. Ibid., 18.

Dr. J. H. Oldham invited her to be a collaborator on *The Christian News-Letter*, a response to the crisis of war. The first issue of *The Christian Newsletter* appeared dated 18th October 1939. Sayers was one of four women in the group which represented the Roman Catholic, Anglican and Free Church traditions. The *News-Letter* had an explicitly ecumenical purpose: "If an adventurous Christian faith is to bring hope and renewal to a decaying civilisation, the first thing to be done is to pool our available resources of Christian understanding and insight."[18] As her first contribution, Sayers agreed to write the Christmas supplement for 1939. It was titled "Is this He that should come?" This article, like her Nativity play, seeks to rip away the veil of religious sentimentality which falsifies our knowledge of Christ. William Temple, the Archbishop of York read this and wrote to Dr. Oldham, "How magnificent Dorothy Sayers is!"[19]

The period from September 1939 till the spring of 1940 is known as the "phoney war." The government had planned on the assumption that fighting would begin immediately. The evacuation from the cities had taken place, and the government's plans seemed to display some fatal flaws that the lack of direct engagement with the enemy highlighted. Sayers wrote "Prevention is better than Cure" in the *St Martin's Review* of December 1939, which recognised that the evacuation seemed, under the present circumstances, to be unnecessary. She reminds the readers that it would be foolish and dangerous to try to do it again when the Germans were actually attacking. More importantly, she saw that the point of aerial bombardment of civilians was to disrupt the national life and panic the population. If the precautions meant the enemy held his hand, then the civilian would have done an exceedingly important thing. She links the responsibility of the citizen for blacking out, for keeping his head and his temper and all the other war-time requirements and links them to her concern for winning the peace as well as the war: "But if we really want nothing [peace] (in that sense) to happen it will not do just to sit back and take no notice; we must be perpetually active and vigilant; we must *make* things not happen. . . . 'Blessed are the peace-makers,' said one who was brought up a carpenter; not 'the peaceable' but 'the peace-*makers*.'"[20]

She used the correspondence column in *The Spectator* to once again challenge the idea of Christianity as a moral system, burdened by outdated

18. Oldham, *Christian Newsletter* 1.

19. Brabazon, *Sayers*, 188.

20. Sayers, "Prevention," 548.

dogma. "The Alternatives before Society" correspondence was a debate between Sayers and those holding what she calls the Jesuanist position, which is that Jesus was a great moral teacher but not God. She claimed that Christianity said he was indeed God. The time she gave to an exchange of letters in the press shows the centrality of Christology in Sayers' religious thinking, and her dedication to parading the Christian flag ostentatiously down the street.

She returned to fiction and published "The Wimsey Papers," "being war-time letters and documents of the Wimsey family" in *The Spectator* from November 17, 1939 until January 19, 1940. In keeping with the characters, the letters were not theological, except for one sermon by The Rev. Theodore Venables, from *The Nine Tailors*, reminding his readers that Christ said more about peace than the Sermon on the Mount and calling on them to take responsibility for making the world better.[21] This form allowed her the freedom to make the criticisms and suggestions that she would have made officially, in a much more palatable and powerful form.

She gave rules for pedestrians walking in the blackout, as well as a suggestion that the omnibuses should place the number at the side of the bus to prevent people darting out in front of it to find out its number. In January 1940 she again used Paul Delgardie as a mouthpiece for expressing her concern at the government's inaction in building public support for France: "I am distressed by the failure of all our public bodies and national organs to forge any links of sympathy between ourselves and the French people at this important juncture. . . . Neither in the newspapers, nor in broadcasting, nor in any other way do I detect any attempt to make Britain aware of France nor yet to recommend Britain to the French."[22]

Throughout the papers she called for people to take responsibility, think about the future. The series concluded with a letter from Peter to Harriet: "You are a writer—there is something you must tell the people, but it is difficult to express. . . . Tell them, this is a battle of a new kind, and it is they who have to fight it, and they must do it themselves and alone. They must not continually ask for leadership—they must lead themselves."[23]

21. Sayers, "Wimsey II," 737.

22. Sayers, "Wimsey X," 105–6. In February 1940 Hilda Matheson of the BBC did write to Sayers asking for a talk to be broadcast to the French. See Suzanne Bray's "Introduction," for an account of the correspondence and Sayers' response.

23. Ibid., 106.

Her publisher, Victor Gollancz asked her to write a Christmas message to the nation. Instead of yet another Nativity meditation, or an uplifting pamphlet, which is probably what he had in mind, she responded with a book *Begin Here* (1939). Before the direct fighting in Britain had begun she was looking beyond the war and writing about winning the peace. *The Church Times* described the book as lucid and helpful summary of the ideas from two works: Peter Drucker's *The End of Economic Man* and the Rev. V.A. Demant's *The Religious Prospect*.[24] She wrote a grand meta-narrative of the changes in the conception of man from Theological Man of the Middle Ages and the revolt against that conception which followed: man as a value in himself (humanist man), man as embodied intelligence (rational man), man as intelligent animal (biological man), man as member of the herd (sociological man), man as response to environment (psychological man), and man the response to the means of livelihood (economic man). Any post-War reconstruction must first get the conception of man right, socialists, fascists, liberals and communists being equally trapped within the conception of economic man. The point of the book was that every citizen needed to think about these issues, and not leave it to the professionals whether religious or secular.

The book was welcomed by Roman Catholic writers as well as Anglicans. The Dominican journal, *Blackfriars* said: "*Blackfriars* readers will have been prepared by "The Greatest Drama" and "Strong Meat" to expect much of this longer essay and they will not be disappointed."[25] *The Tablet's* editor, Douglas Woodruff, was enthusiastic about *Begin Here*. Both reviewers criticized her handling of the Fall as the emergence of self-consciousness identified with the knowledge of good and evil. This does not sufficiently account for the loss of the preternatural grace, and results in a weakness in Sayers' treatment of sacramentality. Fr. Vann's review recognizes the central issue of the book, "The root criticism of our civilisation is that it is causing men and women to become uncreative;" the issue which she grapples with more thoroughly in *The Mind of the Maker*.

In February 1940 the Bishop of Derby, the Rt. Rev. Alfred Edward John Rawlinson, asked her to address the Church Tutorial Classes Association to be held in May of that year. She obliged with an address, "Creed or

24. Both works were on the annotated bibliography of further reading which concluded *Begin Here*.

25. Vann, *Begin Here*, 198.

Chaos?"[26] This address summarises her insights gained when writing "The Greatest Drama," "The Triumph of Easter" and "The Dogma is the Drama" and applying them to the Church's task in the war. The present war, she claimed "in a visible and physical form which we cannot possibly overlook, [is] the final consequences of a quarrel about dogma."[27] She described the condition of the churches in England, with the exception of the Roman Catholic Church, as being one of general toleration, with a disregard for dogma, a vague sentimental attachment to Jesus, and a pious hope that people would follow Christian ethics.

She wrote, "Christian doctrine is not a set of rules, but one vast interlocking rational structure" and there were "seven 'key-positions', namely God, man, sin, judgment, matter, work, and society" which can be worked out from that dogma.[28] She contrasted the Church's s deeply pessimistic view of human nature with the belief in progress that the humanists claimed, and showed that "the Christian Church now finds herself called upon to proclaim the old and hated doctrine of sin as a gospel of cheer and encouragement" to a generation held "fast in the chains of an iron determinism."[29] She addressed the question of work, writing, "The unsacramental attitude of modern society to man and matter is probably closely connected with its unsacramental attitude to work."[30]

This address is remarkable for the amount of theological ground covered in readable prose. It made a public stir attracting attention in the secular and the Roman Catholic press as well as in the Anglican circles which could be expected to be interested in the conference. I believe that this particular work, combined with the popularity of her radio play and her participation in *The Christian Newsletter* led to her being regarded as one of the most able Christian thinkers of her day.

In May 1940, the Minutes of the Executive Committee of the Industrial Christian Fellowship report that the Archbishop of York, William Temple, was planning a conference which was to be held "from September 30th–October 3rd to consider the contribution of the Church to the

---

26. The address was delivered on 4th May 1940 and first published as a pamphlet by Hodder and Stoughton on 10 June 1940. Later it was included in the book *Creed or Chaos? and Other Essays* published by Methuen in February 1947.

27. Sayers, *Creed*, 27.

28. Ibid., 37.

29. Ibid., 41.

30. Ibid., 43.

new world order now emerging. . . The Archbishop of York's Conference would also be confined to members of the Church of England."[31] Given the publicity surrounding "Creed of Chaos?" and the favourable reception Dr. Temple had given Sayers' supplement to the *Christian Newsletter* it is not at all surprising that she was one of the ten speakers invited to present papers at the Conference.[32]

May 1940 was a dark time for Britain. Norway and Denmark had fallen, France was under attack. In the letter to Dr. Oldham, 20 May 1940, she thanks him for his kind comments on "Creed or Chaos?" and apologises for not producing a promised paper on the Rights of Man. She admits that one of the things that is delaying her work is fear: "In plain language, we have all been very much frightened and one does not work well in fright."[33] It is typical of Sayers, though, that she continued to work though frightened and used the opportunity of contributing to *Time and Tide's* Notes on the Way columns. On 15 June 1940 she wrote about Mr. Churchill's becoming Prime Minister, and on Dunkirk. In her contribution for 22 June she returns to the theme of good and evil, judgment and redemption: "The tragic defect [in human nature] is not merely vice; it is the disruption at the core of virtue, which is what the theologians of crisis mean when they exasperate the thoughtless by hammering away at the doctrine of original sinfulness. They are warning him, not so much to dismiss his vices as to distrust his virtues."[34]

She moved from the general to the specific, money and the profit motive. She remarks that economics confuses the creative artist, because the kind of work people do is not discussed. What is particularly interesting about this essay, especially to us in the aftermath of the global financial crisis, is the final paragraph:

> There is a judgment for the artistic temperament also. I have known people who could not be interested in anything except Money—not for what it would buy, but for its own sake. This suggests that the financier is the artist gone wrong, mystically worshipping work for the sake of work, and money for money's sake in a pure exercise of creative fancy. If so, this is fresh proof

31. Temple Archive, Document 4011:183–84.

32. The other speakers were The Rev. W. G. Peck, Mr. M.B. Reckitt, Mr. D. M Mackinnon, The Rev. V. A. Demant, Sir Richard Acland, M.P., Mr. Kenneth Ingram, Mr. J. Middleton Murry, Mr. T. S. Eliot, and the Archbishop of York, William Temple.

33. Sayers, *Letters Vol. 2*, 166.

34. Sayers, "Notes" 22 June, 657.

that the irresponsible artist is a very dangerous fellow; and that any art which cuts itself off from the human soul and the material universe is taking the primrose way to the everlasting bonfire.[35]

She was writing these essays as she was working on *The Mind of the Maker,* and the quoted paragraph shows how widely she tested her own ideas about creativity and work.

Rev. Eric Fenn, Dr. Welch's assistant at the BBC, wrote to her in June asking for two talks to be broadcast in August. She reluctantly agreed and gave a two talk series entitled "Creed or Chaos." The first talk, "The Christ of the Creeds," begins with the firm statement "I am not going to offer you any brand-new theology of my own . . . [but] what the universal Church thinks."[36] The second talk, "The Sacrament of Matter," is a strong defence of the material world, and her central point, "All abuse of matter, or of body and mind, is sacrilege, and a crucifixion of the body of Christ."[37]

She turned down a request from William Temple, then Archbishop of York, to write a play for the Youth Council, because of the pressure of the plays on the life of Christ. If the BBC rejects her first play, she will reconsider. She also expressed her struggle with the speech she is to give at the Archbishop's conference. In words that echo *The Mind of the Maker* she wrote:

> In spite of Mr. Kirk's pleading for practical suggestions, I don't know that I can offer much of a 'solution.' Everybody wants 'solutions' to world problems, as though they were some kind of detective story and by some simple trick you can discover [one] and there you are.[38]

The war's disruption of normal life, and particularly the fall of France, required church leaders to act in innovative ways. Cardinal Hinsley, a Yorkshire man, was concerned to find that Catholics were viewed with suspicion, for Italy was an enemy of Britain, and France had fallen. Cardinal Hinsley used his opportunities for radio addresses and speeches to make clear that he and his fellow Catholics were loyal to Britain. His lay movement, The Sword of the Spirit,[39] was designed to energize Catholics to consider the

35. Ibid., 658.

36. Sayers, *Christ*, 31. Her concept of the universal Church was all Churches which profess the Creeds of Christendom.

37. Ibid., 41.

38. Sayers, *Letters Vol. 2*, 177.

39. For an account of the Sword of the Spirit movement, see M. J. Walsh, *From Sword*

issues of war and post-war reconstruction. This organisation was headed by Cardinal Hinsley with Christopher Dawson as its Vice President, Barbara Ward and A.C. Beales as joint secretaries, and Fr. John Murray S. J. the editor of *The Month*, as one of the theological overseers. The organization's first effort was to organise study groups throughout the nation. The suggested reading material for the groups included two works by Sayers: *Creed or Chaos?* and *Begin Here*.

The next significant step in ecumenical progress was the letter published on 21 December 1940 in the *Times* signed by the Anglican Archbishops Lang and Temple, Cardinal Hinsley and the Moderator of the Free Church Federal Council, Walter H. Armstrong. This letter endorsed Pope Pius XII's five peace points and five points from the Oxford Conference of 1937.[40] This was unprecedented and marked a broadening of the ecumenical fraternity.

Because of the Blitz, the Archbishop of York's conference, The Life of the Church and the Order of Society, convened at Malvern in January, 1941. This conference was wholly Anglican, but with the leadership of Temple and Bell, it looked beyond the established Church to the wider world, that of other churches and of secular society. Sayers' invitation can be attributed to Temple's appreciation for her work. Sayers' speech for the conference was titled "The Church's Responsibility" and was to answer two questions:

1. Is the Church's witness concerned with the possibility of a breakdown of civilization, and with the economic and political causes of such a breakdown? If so, upon what grounds?

2. Does the present situation derive in any degree from the fact that the modern church has been more concerned to raise the moral level of social effort rather than to discover and correct falsity in the dominant purposes of corporate life?

Sayers' talk was an exercise in creative ecclesiology. She defines what she means by Church: "A body of men, living in the world, united in a recognizable and conscious fellowship and organized within a living tradition whose essence persists unchanged while its expressions continually

---

to Ploughshare; Hastings, *History of English Christianity 1920–2000*; Moloney, *Westminster, Whitehall and the Vatican.*

40. The text of the letter is printed in Appendix I.

develop, by a single devotion and a single service to an immanent and transcendent reality, whose claims are felt to be paramount."[41]

She notes that this definition can be criticized because it does not state where the union comes from, the members or the reality which transcends them. This consideration was outside the analogy she was going to draw which, she said, worked whether the attitude to that question was "Pelagian, Calvinist, or Catholic."[42] She proposed two models of church, the theater or the Nazi party, which she described as "a mystical, fanatical and authoritarian Church—idolatrous and evil . . . but nevertheless real and living."[43] The working out of her argument depends on the Incarnation: "If . . . the Church, as a Christian society, is concerned with civilization, or with politics and economics, it can only be on the grounds of a realistic and sacramental theology of the Incarnation."[44] Having established a sacramental position to argue for the Church's concern with the breakdown of civilization, her first question to answer, she goes on to the second: the relation of morality and truth. Here she criticises the church heavily for concentrating on the sins of the bedroom and cooperating meekly with economics. Her conclusion asks the Church to have integrity, "I do not mean that she must be uninterested in the social, political and moral sphere of the Law, but that she must be disinterested."[45]

She goes on to elaborate what such integrity would require with reference especially to the arts. The secular press fastened on her contrast of true integrity to current morality: "Suppose, during the last century, the Churches had devoted to sweetening intellectual corruption one quarter of the energy they spent on nosing out fornication—or denounced legalized cheating with one quarter of the vehemence with which they denounced legalized adultery? . . . if every man living were to sleep in his neighbour's bed, it could not bring the world so near shipwreck as that pride, that avarice, and that intellectual sloth which the Church has forgotten to write in the tale of the capital Sins."[46]

Sayers public appearances, from the Malvern conference onwards, concentrated on speeches about point nine in the joint ecumenical letter,

41. Sayers, "Church's Responsibility," 37–38.
42. Ibid.
43. Ibid., 60.
44. Ibid.
45. Ibid., 73.
46. Ibid., 72–73.

"Restoring the sense of Divine vocation to work." She has four major presentations on work and vocation. In March 1941 she spoke at Bishop Bell's request at the Dome in Brighton[47], in April she wrote a long letter (see Appendix II) to *The Catholic Herald* explaining her dogmatic foundation for that speech, in May 1941 she spoke at the interfaith meeting organized by the Sword in the Spirit group, and in 1942 she spoke at Eastbourne.

The Sword of the Spirit organized a follow-up meeting to the *Times* letter. Barbara Ward's letter of invitation to Bishop George Bell to speak at the meeting mentions that Sayers has been invited to speak.[48] Michael Walsh recounts that "The Sword executive especially requested that the Cardinal approve a woman speaker, preferably Miss Dorothy Sayers. Hinsley concurred."[49] The speakers for the two meetings were a distinguished lot: On Saturday 10 May with Cardinal Hinsley in the chair, Bishop Bell, Richard O'Sullivan Q.C. and Hugh Lyon, headmaster of Rugby spoke on "A Christian International Order." On the Sunday with Archbishop Lang presiding, Dr Sidney Berry, Acting Moderator of the Free Church Council, Christopher Dawson, Sayers and Fr. Martin D'Arcy S.J. spoke on "A Christian Order for Britain."

The meetings took place in the Stoll Theatre, which was filled to capacity, variously reported as 2000–3000 seats. On the Saturday night, 10th May, London suffered the worst night of the war: the House of Commons was destroyed; Westminster Abbey, Westminster Hall, Lambeth Palace, Charterhouse, and the British Museum were all gravely damaged. Despite this, the Sunday meeting also attracted a full house. The meetings and speeches were reported in the secular and religious press. Dr. Oldham's *Christian News-Letter* reported the meetings "gave expression to a growing common understanding among Christians of all communions of the menace to-day to all that Christianity stands for and of the need of a common front to overcome it."[50] Sayers was to speak on the restoration of a sense of divine vocation to work. The *Church Times* reported: "The Archbishop [Lang] introduced Miss Dorothy L. Sayers with a reference to 'that aristocratic relation of hers, Lord Peter,' but hastened to commend her in her own right as

47. This speech was abridged and published in *Bulletins from Britain* and in *A Christian Basis for the Post-War World* (Sayers, "Vocation in Work") from which citations are taken.

48. Bell, Volume 71/46.

49. Walsh, *From Sword to Ploughshare*, 8.

50. Oldham, *The Christian Newsletter*, 28 May 1941.

'a most courageous and forceful Christian speaker and thinker.' Miss Sayers abundantly justified His Grace's encomiums in a brilliant exposition of life and work as they are, and as they ought to be in a Christian civilisation."[51]

The Tablet commented that: "We would have preferred to see the vital issue of the restoration of a sense of vocation to men's daily work put in the first place. . . . Here is a very real field in which the combined influence of the Christian bodies can bring its weight to bear, to break down the opposite entrenched idea that a man is to be judged and valued not at all according to the way he makes his money, but only according to the use he puts it to after making it."[52]

She gave many other speeches which were often reported in the local press, such as her speech at St Martin's-in-the-Fields on work and leisure.[53]

Sayers returned to the theme of vocation in work at Eastbourne in April 1942, which was published by Methuen in a pamphlet titled *Why Work?* In all of her speeches and writing about work there is a consistent argument. Unlike those who see humanity's highest vocation in leisure, Sayers sees our vocation in work. Man is *homo faber*; he bears the image of God in his ability and desire to create.[54] This desire is frustrated in the modern industrial system in which work becomes work to escape work. We should look to the artists (and others such as scientists and craftsmen) for work that fits human nature, which is work that the worker lives to do. The same divide is found in leisure: one group of humanity which includes the idle rich and idle women, seeks leisure for escape, to kill time; the second group sees leisure as a rest which enables them to work again.[55] The Church should form Christian men and women in dogma and Christian ethical principles and then respect their autonomy to work in the world.[56] The work should suit the talents of the worker[57] whether male or female.[58] A right kind of work must be related not only to the right understanding of the needs of man but also a willingness to serve and love the material

51. *Church Times*, "Call," 282.

52. *The Tablet*, Editorial, 384.

53. *Mid-Sussex Times*, "Miss Sayers," 1, *Church Times*, "Tirade," 101.

54. Sayers, "Vocation," 89.

55. Ibid., 92; "Work," 1; Sayers, *Unpopular Opinions*, 123.

56. Sayers, *Why Work?* 17; "Work" 8–9.

57. Sayers, *Creed*, 56.

58. Sayers, *Unpopular Opinions*, 109.

body of God's universe.[59] The worker should serve the work not the community.[60] Work should be organised so that it provides opportunity for individual initiative, allows the worker to see a final result of their labour and fits with the rhythm of the human body.[61] Her argument depended on her understanding of the Trinity and of the Incarnation, so it is a theological ethic of work. How important the theological conceptions were can be seen from the project she undertook in 1941, while she was completing *The Mind of the Maker* and preparing for the speech at Eastbourne.

In October 1941, Sayers sent Dr. Welch a copy of her letter to Count Michael de la Bedoyère, editor of the *Catholic Herald* and author of *Christian Crisis*, proposing an ecumenical effort at a book stating the "Highest Common Factor" of agreement between the Churches, which Sayers nicknamed the "Oecumenical Penguin." This project interested Welch, who contacted Cardinal Hinsley. The Cardinal, suffering, in Sayers' view, from the stiff theologians that Cardinal Bourne had imposed on the Diocese of Westminster, was not keen. He had been unable to persuade his theologians or his brother bishops that Christian co-operation, especially that which included any common prayer, was tolerable. Indeed for the first annual meeting of the Sword of the Spirit in August 1941, he had to impose a new constitution that stipulated that only Catholics could be full members and that the organisation was to be under the control of the diocesan bishop.

When Sayers stayed with Bishop Bell in April 1942 on the occasion of her speech in Eastbourne, the discussion must have touched on this project. In her thank you letter to Mrs. Bell Sayers enclosed a copy of the memorandum she had written proposing this Oecumenical Penguin with a note "for the Bishop's amusement."[62] Bishop Bell was interested and asked to see the full correspondence which he then sent on to Archbishop Temple, now occupying the see of Canterbury. Temple gave the project his support, including guaranteeing Sayers' requested fee of £50. Canon Quick, Regius Professor of Divinity at Oxford was to lead the group of theologians. The project never succeeded, but it did produce three memoranda from Sayers now held in the Bell archives at Lambeth Palace which illustrate her breadth of theological knowledge, her appreciation of the difficulties of Christian co-operation with the Roman Catholic Church, her appreciation

59. Sayers, "Vocation," 102.

60. Sayers, *Why Work?* 19.

61. Sayers, *Unpopular Opinions*, 125.

62. See Bell, vol. 208/257.

of the problems in conveying doctrine to modern man, and the common misunderstandings theological language produces when used without explanations. It is worth noting that Canon Quick and the other theologians found no major faults in Sayers' memoranda except her proposal that the Oecumenical Penguin could be used as a syllabus for schools. The question of religious education was a battleground of warring factions and Canon Quick warned in his first letter to Temple that for the project to succeed, any suggestion of involvement in the religious education debate must be avoided.

One of the difficulties was that the mutual expectations were not clear. The theologians wanted Sayers to produce a document which they would comment on; Sayers wanted the theologians to produce a document that she could translate into current language. In a letter to Temple, Sayers suggests that she take the project to London, to people who will help her create a draft. Temple agreed.

The people in London were most likely the Rev. Patrick McLaughin and the Rev. Gilbert Shaw at St. Anne's Soho. They were trying to address intellectuals in their own language and present the claims of Christianity to them for serious consideration. Sayers spoke on drama at the first mission, during the summer of 1943 which was titled "Christian Faith and Contemporary Culture." The speakers included, among others, T. S. Eliot on literature, Lady Rhondda from *Time and Tide* on journalism and Dr. Welch from the BBC on broadcasting. Sayers produced a major speech, later published as a pamphlet, for another mission entitled *Making Sense of the Universe,* which once again proposed Christianity as an intellectual framework which proposes to give a coherent, consistent account of life.

She had begun refusing speaking engagements which asked her to speak on religion, and refused Temple's offer of a Lambeth D.D. She discovered Dante, and was absorbed in her new interest, fired by Charles William's *The Figure of Beatrice,* from 1944 until the end of her life. In the years she was participating in the public discussion of Christianity, she made major contributions, and to evaluate them, we need to see Sayers within the context of Anglican Social Ethics, and its great figure, William Temple. It was Temple's appreciation of Sayers which gave her such a prominent place, particularly at the Malvern Conference.

Anglican Social Ethics

Sayers enters the tradition of Anglican Social Ethics at the Malvern Conference in 1941, at the invitation of William Temple, then Archbishop of York.
Sayers was not part of Church organisations, academic faculties of theology, theological discussion circles or groups at that time other than participating as a contributor to *The Christian News-Letter* and as a member of the
Catholic Writers Guild, about which we have little information other than
the connection with the Rev. Patrick McLaughlin, later of St Anne's, Soho.
She divided her time between Witham and London, meeting her friends
who came from literary and theatrical circles. The invitation to speak at
Malvern was a mark of her stature as a Christian writer and thinker, and of
Temple's appreciation of her work.

Temple, the convenor of the Malvern Conference and subsequently
the Archbishop of Canterbury, is the major figure of Anglican social ethics
of his day. He is significant to this book because of his recognition of Sayers'
gifts and because he shared with her a commitment to natural theology and
ethical reasoning in the natural law tradition. He offers an example of the
vibrancy of Anglican philosophy in the early years of the twentieth century
and how important reason was in Anglican theology along with Scripture
and Tradition. Michael Ramsey described Temple as someone who "came
to theology from philosophy in a journey through several stages; and in a
sense his theology was that of an amateur."[63] He stands in the tradition of
liberal Christianity that sought to reconcile Christian revelation with the
new discoveries in cosmology, anthropology and the changed conditions
of life after the industrial revolution. Ramsey recounts Temple's describing
his method to Ronald Knox, "I am not asking what Jones will swallow: I am
Jones asking what there is to eat."[64]

Temple's philosophical questioning meant that he was refused ordination by Bishop Paget of Oxford because of Temple's doubts about the
creed. He was not prepared to accept the Virgin Birth or the Resurrection
as simply given. Two years later he again asked for ordination, this time to
Archbishop Davidson. Davidson was interested in the trend of Temple's
thought and wrote to Paget recommending his ordination, "I do not say
that he expresses himself respecting either truth with the distinctness (at
least as to detail) which has been usual in orthodox theology. But I can

63. Ramsey, *From Gore to Temple*, 146.
64. Ibid., 7.

see no adequate reason why he should not now be ordained."[65] At the time Davidson recommended him for ordination, Temple accepted that the evidence for the Resurrection outweighed the difficulties of accepting it. In his later years he became convinced of the congruity of the Virgin Birth with the Incarnation. In his popular preaching he would say: "To believe in miracle is to take divine personality in deadly earnest."[66]

Ramsey credits Randall Davidson for saving for Anglicanism one who was to become foremost in the exposition of orthodoxy and creedal miracles, and cites this incident as showing the Anglican vocation – "to risk untidiness and rough edges and apparently insecure fences so that it may be in and through the intellectual turmoil of the time—and not in aloofness from it—that the Church teaches the Catholic faith."[67] Rowan Williams would agree; he characterises the liberal Anglican theological style as a scepticism, "about formulae and dogma that is fundamentally scepticism about the capacities of the human mind. . . . In this context, to be cautious about hermeneutical or dogmatic closure is not to discard or relativise sanctioned words; you occupy the territory marked out by those words, but you will not know where the boundaries are, because the search for definite boundaries suggests that you might be 'in possession' of the territory, not yourself included in (possessed by?) it."[68]

Craig writes that three concepts—natural law, the value of human personality and man as a sinner—deepened in Temple's latter years and made his analysis of the human situation more realistic.[69]

The great divide within Anglicanism in the years before the First World War was the question, "Does the Church have the right to comment on politics and the economy?" Temple strongly affirmed that the church did have that right; he held a sacramental view of the relation of spirit to matter. Temple was a major figure in each of the great events which mark the stages of Anglican Social Ethics in the twentieth century. He "was committed in 1908 to socialism as the economic realization of the Christian gospel, but moved in the 1930s to a more realistic position."[70] Temple was the youngest member of the Archbishops' Commission on Church and State in 1916,

---

65. Ibid., 88–89.
66. Ibid., 89.
67. Ibid., 89.
68. Williams, *Anglican Identities*, 81.
69. Craig, *Social Concern*, 124.
70. Sedgwick, "Christian Teaching," 219.

Chairman of Interdenominational Conference on Politics, Economics, and Citizenship (COPEC) in 1924, a speaker at the Oxford Conference on Church, Community and State in July 1937 and Chairman of the Edinburgh conference on Faith and Order in August 1937 and convenor of the Malvern Conference in 1941. Adrian Hastings says of him that "he provided leadership as no one else in the Christian Church of the twentieth century has quite managed to do. He gave it not only to the Church of England but in an increasingly wide measure to the whole Christian ecumene."[71]

The major features and development of Anglican social ethics become apparent through the events in which Temple participated. The Fifth Report of the Archbishops' Commission (COPEC) had five major points: 1) Christian moral teaching applies as much to society, industry, and economics as to the individual. 2) The New Testament teaching about the dangers of wealth is to be emphasized. 3) Men must never be regarded as mere instruments of production. 4) Christianity's high regard for the individual is complemented by its insistence on the duty of service in corporate life, and 5) Society must accept responsibility for the welfare of its members.[72]

The COPEC conference in 1924 came, as the Rev. Charles Raven later wrote, at a particularly favourable moment, between the fall of fundamentalism and the rise of Barthianism and the theology of crisis. Temple identified the Christian principles behind any programme of social ethics as the sacredness of personality, the brotherhood of men, the duty of service, and the way of sacrifice.[73] The conference ended on a generally optimistic note, and the gap between COPEC in 1924 and the Oxford and Edinburgh Conferences of 1937 was marked by the failure of the League of Nations, the world-wide financial crisis and depression, and the rise of Nazism. Raven, commenting on what he called the essential weakness of the work of COPEC wrote: "We had relied upon selected biblical texts rather than any relevant theology; when applied to the new cosmology, anthropology, psychology and sociology of the twentieth century our equipment though less archaic than that of Christendom in general, could not stand the strain. We had no understanding of the modern technological world-wide aggregates, productive of benefits which we could not wisely use and evils which no

71. Hastings, *History*, 256.

72. Oliver, *Church and Social Order*, 49.

73. Ibid., 68.

one individual could restrain or cure. . . . Rome at least had a philosophy of corporate life, even if it was identified with an institutional anachronism."[74]

A theological revolution as well as events challenged the Anglicans between COPEC and Oxford: "The next orthodoxy derived from the bleak Calvinistic dogma of the total depravity of the world supplemented by exaggeration of the Lutheran doctrines of the state and of salvation by faith alone, and interpreted by Kierkegaard, Barth and in a popular form by Reinhold Niebuhr, swept over the Channel and the Atlantic to destroy the ancient Christian Platonism of the British Churches."[75]

The Oxford Conference on Church, Community and State in July 1937 lasted two weeks and attracted over 800 participants. The event was reported daily in *The Times*, with accounts of the debates over pacifism, the position of the German confessing church, the profit motive, and other economic questions. Some at the conference criticized the economic system for, "the denial of the Christian's call to do the will of God in his daily work implied in forced unemployment and in some actual forms of employment; the powerlessness of the investor and consumer to control the results of their economic behaviour."[76]

The article went on to report the dissent at the conference: The Archdeacon of Monmouth, the Ven. A. E. Monahan, protested that there was no condemnation of Communism and Fascism. J. M Speers, a New York businessman, claimed that the assumption that the existing economic order was opposed to Christianity was unsupported. Paul Tillich in response asked the conference to listen to the voice of God speaking to the church even through the Communist movement.[77]

This conference produced two documented outcomes. The first was of more significance to the ecumenical movement than to Anglican social ethics: to establish in union with Faith and Order a World Council of Churches.[78] The second was in the field of social ethics: the resolutions of the conference formed half of the letter "Foundations of Peace" which had appeared in *The Times* 21 December 1940.[79] Theologically, perhaps, the greatest advance was the new recognition that original sin is a social fact

---

74. Raven, "COPEC," 12.

75. Ibid., 13.

76. *The Times*, "Report on Oxford," 9.

77. Ibid.

78. Hastings, *History*, 305.

79. Ibid., 392. See Appendix I.

governing all other facts, and the experience of confronting totalitarianism which overrode all individuality and freedom of individuals.[80]

In addition to the conference, two important works in this tradition appeared in the 1930s: *The Challenge of the Slums* produced by Bishop Garbett in 1933, and *Men without Work*, a report on unemployment by the Pilgrim Trust in 1938. Hastings reports of the latter that it:

> had been produced by a team of enquirers established by a Committee on Unemployment brought together by Temple and including Bishop Bell, Lindsay of Balliol, Sir Walter Moberly and J. H. Oldham. The importance for us of this document is not just the subject but the efficiency with which it was tackled. It has generally been recognized as the "best social study of unemployment made in the thirties." . . . for the first time outside the field of education, it had moved from an amateur to a fully professional model in approaching a social problem. *Men Without Work* limited the frontiers of its subject and made a lasting contribution which the COPEC reports of ten years earlier had too obviously failed to do.[81]

Malvern was the last great public conference organized and presided over by Temple. It was organized by the Industrial Christian Fellowship, the church body which replaced the Christian Social Union, with large input from the *Christendom* Group.[82] Suggate remarks that, "Not only did Temple and his *Christendom* Group friends engage with natural law as part of an important search for deeper foundations in the face of world crisis; at the same time many Catholics on the Continent found in natural law a practical defence of the person against totalitarianism."[83]

Temple made his allegiance to the catholic tradition clear in his introduction to the Malvern Conference, "We approach our task as Anglicans, that is, as heirs of the whole richness of Catholic tradition and also of the special insights of the Reformation. And here a great choice must be made: Do we or do we not follow the Reformers in their rejection of all Natural

---

80. Lloyd, *Church of England*, 306.

81. Hastings, *History*, 57–58.

82. This group was led by Maurice Reckitt, Dr. William Peck, Ruth Kenyon, and Canon V. A. Demant. Their journal *Christendom* sought to develop a Christian sociology and the group was strongly committed to the social credit ideas of Douglas, as well as to a natural law ethic, guild organisation for industry, a family wage rather than contraception, and nationalism rather than internationalism.

83. Suggate, *William Temple*, 106.

Theology? If we reject that view [Machiavelli's and Luther's that the state is independent of God] and believe that there is a truth about the political and social life of man which is at once divine in essence (for man is God's creature) and apprehensible by reason, we shall do well to start with the great scholastics."[84] Temple was not one of the followers of Barth. He found Barthian theology heretical, with its hard and fast distinction between reason and revelation, and incapable of serving as a relevant critic of the issues of social and political life.[85]

Sayers' contribution to Malvern, an exercise in creative ecclesiology and interpretation of the integrity and autonomy of the secular sphere, was discussed above. She spoke from her usual position, a layperson engaged with the world who accepted Christian dogma and tried to make sense of her experiences in light of that dogma. Skilled as she was in translation, she understood dogma as a framework for understanding. When faced with an apparent conflict between dogma and modern science, for example, she first looked at the language being used, and examined the philosophical underpinnings of it. She shared a commitment to natural theology and its concomitant ethics of the natural law, although as she was not a philosopher and so did not express a very academic version of either. She made them the assumptions from which she reasoned.

Temple, possessing as he did a doctrine of the State as well as of the Church, was ready as a social thinker to trace the lines of a divine order of society, and as the ground for this he turned increasingly to the concept of natural law. He saw natural law as giving the key to the proper functions of state, family, property and trade.[86]

Malvern was not a gathering of the like-minded. There were those, like Sayers, who were sympathetic to the *Christendom* Group and who held a natural law ethic but who were not committed to the other ideas of the group, particularly the social credit ideas of Douglas or the fascination with medieval life and a wish to return to the guild system and small communities. Others, including younger theologians influenced by Barth,[87] were hostile to the *Christendom* Group's ideas on theology, ethics and social

---

84. Sayers, "Church's Responsibility," 12–13.

85. Craig, *Social Concern*, 152.

86. Ramsey, *From Gore to Temple*, 154.

87. Ramsey describes the impact of Barth's theology in England: "It was the 'shock' of facing, with a starkness we had not seen before, the contrasts: God—Man, Creator—Creature, God—World." Ibid., 142.

organisation. There were advocates of the abolition of private ownership as a necessary part of any program of Christian social ethics, and were represented by Sir Richard Ingram. Temple's genius was to be able to show this diverse group what agreement they shared, and to give them the liberty to disagree and keep discussing other points. This agreement, though, was not without problems: the editor of the Supplement to *Crockford's Clerical Directory* found the recommendations from Malvern to be so general as to be unobjectionable. He goes on, however, to object strongly to the conference's distrust of the profit motive, stating "The 'Profit Motive' is entirely legitimate and up to a point actively beneficial. But like many other good things (e.g. a liking for beer) it must be kept within bounds."[88]

In two articles in *The Modern Churchman*, the Rev. Ronald Preston analyses the Malvern Conference of 1941, and one hundred years Anglican Social ethics generally. He sees three wings in the church with varying commitment to social ethics in the 1800s. The first group were the evangelicals, anti-democratic, individualistic and generally removed from the world. Although they led the anti-slavery campaign and the Sunday school movement, their social outreach was the result, he says, of "individual faith bearing fruit in works"[89] rather than a coherent social ethic. The second group, the Tractarians, pressed the uniqueness of the church and "With all their personal service and generosity, they, no better than the Evangelicals, got beyond a class-conscious charity."[90] The Broad Church was prepared to engage with modern society, and in 1889 founded the Christian Social Union "to study in common how to apply the moral truths and principles of Christianity to the social and economic difficulties of the present time."[91] As work progressed, "It began to be seen that the form in which Christian ends are realized will vary with different stages in the social process, and the facts of that process must be mastered before it is possible to know what to advocate." [92]

Preston acknowledges the contribution of the Anglo-Catholics along with the major criticism he makes of the *Christendom* group:

> The great bulk of Anglican social thought in the last century has been contributed by Anglo-Catholics. They have tried to develop

88. *Crockfords*, x.
89. Preston, "Century of Anglican Thought," 339.
90. Ibid., 339.
91. Ibid., 343.
92. Ibid.

the social theories of the Middle Ages, which were largely lost because of their inadequacy. . . . Their analysis of modern economics and industry has been inadequate and erroneous because their theology has prevented them from admitting the necessary autonomy of the social sciences and hence from acquiring the specialized technique needed for dealing with the complex modern social scene. Further, their search for some "Christian" alternative to the authoritarian or democratic planning which are the only courses open to us, has meant that they have been remote from the practical issues of the day.[93]

Preston's criticism centers on the idea of natural law that he maintains the *Christendom* group held and expounded at Malvern which, in his opinion, did not recognize the autonomy of the social sciences. He goes on to press the claims of the social sciences as independent and concludes that natural law ethics cannot cope with the modern world.

If natural law is to be rejected altogether, then Temple's social ethics must also be rejected. However, Temple's understanding of natural law was philosophically and theologically nuanced. Temple did not accept the *Christendom* Group's program or think that churchmen should construct a social order. He saw the primary task of the church to make good Christian men and women who will perform their social duties in the world in the light and power of their Christian faith.[94] He sought for conferences such as Malvern to construct "Middle Axioms" between detailed policy prescriptions and general principles. This leaves room for the specialised knowledge of various intellectual disciplines to contribute to the middle axioms and guides the specialist in constructing detailed policies. Since every ethic is based on a conception of the person, theology will have a contribution to that discussion which needs to be complemented by an accurate psychology, sociology and anthropology.

Temple had a realistic view of mankind, and criticised the Thomism of his day, for, among other things, an inadequate understanding of sin as compared to Niebuhr's work in the industrialised economy. Temple didn't think abolishing private property would solve all social ills, but thought that St Thomas had "a most wholesome doctrine much needed in our day, avoiding as it does, the unsocial outlook of the individualist and the socialist's check upon initiative."[95]

93. Ibid., 346–47.
94. Craig, *Social Concern*, 138.
95. Temple, "Thomism," 88.

Preston's summary of Sayers' presentation at Malvern highlights the similarities between her views and Temple's:

> Miss Dorothy Sayers contributes an extremely able and well con-structed paper to argue that the Church must sanctify the whole of human life without, however, identifying itself with any rela-tive and transitory social, political or artistic system. In the course of it she makes an illuminating comparison between the kind of community the Church should be, compared with the intense and narrow fellowship of the actors' world on the one hand and the totalitarian exclusiveness of the Nazi "church" on the other. She ends with a strong plea for intellectual integrity in the Church in all spheres, and especially with regard to the arts.[96]

Sayers, like Temple, held a sacramental view of creation, saw that the Church was not to be identified with any particular social system, and made a strong case for the independence and integrity of all human work. In that connection, it is interesting that her speaking is limited to those things which she does know: the dogma of the Church, what it is she be-lieves; human work and the necessity for human beings made in the image of the Trinitarian creator to create; and religious drama, including liturgy. She didn't offer economic solutions, or endorse the *Christendom* group's adherence to the guild organisation of industry or the social credit model. She did, however, believe that a correct understanding of the human be-ing and work which was suited to that human nature would prove sound economically and theologically.

Sayers spoke at the Malvern Conference primarily as a writer. Her insights on work and her analogy for the Trinity arose through her work as a creative writer. She was part of a society which discussed religious ques-tions freely, with literary figures regularly appearing in newspaper forums or radio broadcasts on "What I believe," and similar topics which Ronald Knox satirised so effectively in *Broadcast Minds*. Apparently this tendency annoyed the editor of *Crockfords* as well, as he comments in the preface in which he had dealt with the Malvern Conference: "A desirable addition to religious education would be a system of elementary classes for budding novelists, so that if in after life they feel impelled to ventilate their opin-ions on Christian theology, philosophy and ethics they should at least have some notion of what they are talking about. Proficiency in the production

96. Preston, "Malvern Conference," 20.

of imaginative fiction ought not to be regarded as equivalent to the training and equipment of a scholar."[97]

We cannot be sure that he was speaking of Sayers, but if so, perhaps he was offended by someone who was still known primarily as a detective novelist, appearing at Malvern and her presuming to talk about ecclesiology. At least some Anglican clergy found her a problematic figure. In May of 1941, after her appearance at the Malvern Conference and the Dome Mission, Bishop Bell received a letter from a clergyman, the Rev. Bouquet, suggesting that Sayers not be put forward as a strong Anglican. Bishop Bell, naturally, requested that he give reasons for this. Bouquet responded:

> my information is confidential through Canon Steele who heard from her former parish priest, Canon Campbell of Witham (who got into the house to see her old mother who was ill—when DLS was in London) . . . also Canon Widdrington [who was] trying to get her to become a communicant member of his C of E . . . [she is] a theoretical Catholic . . . But though I have not the slightest reason to suppose that she is likely to become an RC or that she is not quite sincere—still with the warning of GKC and to some extent of Shelia Kay-Smith in our mind—there is a danger of rushing after celebrities of the moment and being let down.[98]

The hostility of this piece of hearsay is quite amazing. Sayers' mother had died in 1929, a fact Bouquet fails to mention in a letter written in 1941. Bell forwarded the letter to Lang, noting that "it is only a suggestion that one should go slow, I think." Archbishop Lang, responded: "she may be meditating a voyage elsewhere. But apart from that I have lately been thinking that the C of E tended to make too much of her and put her too much in its front window. I will remember what Bouquet has said."[99] Fortunately, William Temple did not share Archbishop Lang's opinion.

What is apparent examining the history of Anglican Social ethics up to and including the Malvern conference is the diversity of theological, philosophical, scientific and political thinking which contribute to the discussion. The theology of Barth was attracting followers among the clergy present at Malvern, and Niebuhr's theology of crisis seemed to many, as it seemed to Temple, to be more relevant to the age than Thomism. Ramsey describes the change in theology from the 1920s to the late 1930's as moving

97. *Crockfords*, xiv.

98. Bell, vol. 208:246–47.

99. Ibid., 248.

from a focus on the Incarnation to a focus on the Redemption.[100] The latter is an acknowledgement of the evil in the world and our need for repentance and redemption. Preston comments that a particular strength of Anglican social ethics of the inter-war period was its ecumenical dimension: "Anglicans are no longer working out a Christian social theory on their own; they are enriched by the contributions of an American Churchman like Reinhold Niebuhr, a Continental Reformed Churchman like Emil Brunner . . . a Greek Orthodox like Nicholas Berdyaev and a Roman Catholic like Jacques Maritain."[101]

Sayers' work towards the Oecumenical Penguin shows her understanding of the problems dealing with a the Roman Catholic Church with its fixed boundaries, unwillingness to compromise on the formulae for doctrine or to seem to validate Christian bodies by participating in shared worship even in the face of the common enemy of Nazism. In her speeches and writing on work, however, she found acceptance and appreciation; even the "stiff" theologians that she told James Welch had been planted on Cardinal Hinsley by Cardinal Bourne had no problems with Catholics cooperating with other Christians in practical action for social change. It was praying together, or having an organisation with equal Catholic and non-Catholic members with the purpose of Christian Social Action that was not permitted.

Sayers quite clearly belongs in the Anglican tradition, and often found the rigidity of the Roman Catholics of her day distasteful. She was fully aware of the Vatican's ill repute among the British for its political settlements with Fascism.[102] When she was working on the Oecumenical Penguin she dealt directly with the problem arising from the Roman attitude which, in the pursuit of the fullness of truth, allowed no distinction between articles of faith which are fundamental and those which are not. She wrote in a memorandum to Canon Quick, "what actually happens is that non-Catholics are led to suppose that the 'disputed' doctrines are *more* [emphasis in original] fundamental and important than the others because of the to-do made about them."[103]

The Roman Catholic tradition of social ethics, like the Anglican tradition of social ethics, was concerned with the conditions of work: wages,

---

100. Ramsey *From Gore to Temple*, 159.

101. Preston, "Century," 345.

102. Sayers, *Letters Vol. 2*, 80.

103. Temple, Correspondence, vol. 39/236.

safety, and the rights of workers to organise; and the problem of unemployment in the industrial economy. Neither tradition questioned the work that people were called to do, except those who advocated a return to small holdings and guilds, a view Sayers rejected. Given the experience of the time with mass unemployment, the exploitation of the workers and the lack of a safety net, it is understandable that the Church should address the immediate and pressing needs of those suffering in the industrialised economy. Sayers may seem to be insensitive to this, but a close reading reveals that she knew her lack of knowledge of macro-economic policy and respected another discipline's boundaries.

Sayers' method in theology, translation, shows that she recognised the differences that existed between historical periods and between adherents of different philosophical world views. Sayers placed herself with the Schoolmen, she used natural law categories and reasoning for her ethics. She becomes an important public Christian through her writing, imaginative and expository. She enters Anglican social ethics as an official participant through the sponsorship of William Temple, especially by her invitation to speak at his Malvern conference.

Looking at the history and variety of philosophical approaches to social ethics at that conference and in the wider tradition of Anglican social ethics, and comparing that to Roman Catholic social ethics of the same period, Sayers and Temple are found to be accepted by Roman Catholics of the day as sharing a tradition of reasoning and having valuable insights. Sayers' work in social ethics was grounded in her theology of the Incarnation and Trinity. It is that theology that is the subject of the next chapter.

4

The Artist and the Trinity

SAYERS' ANALYSIS OF THE crisis facing Europe in 1939 in *Begin Here* was anthropological. Over the course of the twentieth century, the concept of Economic Man, particularly in Marxism, forced the churches and secular thinkers to grapple with its challenge to the traditional understanding of the person. New philosophical thinking in existentialism and personalism centered on this question. Positivist philosophy could not account for persons other than as a bundle of perceptions; or a locus of feelings in emotivist ethics. This philosophy and the anthropology of modernity in the social sciences had removed the transcendent dimension from any understanding of man.

A second anthropological discussion revolved around questions of gender. In the 1920s and 1930s the question of sex differences was strongly debated amongst feminists. Those known as welfare feminists, such as Eleanor Rathbone, accepted that biological differences and different family roles led to different needs, interests and outlets for men and women. Others, now described as equity feminists, such as Winnifred Holtby acknowledged sex differentiation as important, but thought its influence was overstated.[1] Sayers would fall on the equity feminist side of this divide.

Sayers opposed the hierarchical understanding of gender and argued for the position which held that men and women were first and equally

---

1. Caine, *English Feminism,* 215.

human; their differences existed but the differences between individual men and individual women were as important as the supposed "natural" differences between the biological sexes. Sayers was claiming that men and women shared a common humanity in opposition to stereotypes of society which proposed that men and women are two separate, different, and unequal beings.

Sayers' theology of work depends upon her conception of humanity: man is *homo faber*, he bears the image of God in his ability and desire to create.[2] This conception of humanity can rightly be called Sayers' Christian anthropology. Her work *The Mind of the Maker* examines creative mind, the mind that provides an analogy for the Trinity. So Sayers' anthropology is Christian in its fullest sense, it is Trinitarian. Her analogy for the Trinity appeared in its full form in the printed version of the play *The Zeal of Thy House* and was discussed in detail in her book *The Mind of the Maker*. It is,

> Praise Him that He hath made man in His own image, a maker and craftsman like Himself, a little mirror of His triune majesty.
>
> For every work of creation is threefold, an earthly trinity to match the heavenly.
>
> First: there is the Creative Idea; passionless, timeless, beholding the whole work complete at once, the end in the beginning, and this is the image of the Father.
>
> Second, there is the Creative Energy, begotten of that Idea, working in time from the beginning to the end, with sweat and passion, being incarnate in the bonds of matter, and this is the image of the Word.
>
> Third: there is the Creative Power, the meaning of the work and its response in the lively soul; and this is the image of the Spirit.
>
> And these three are one, each equally in itself the whole work, whereof none can exist without the other; and this is the image of the Trinity.[3]

This analogy of the Trinity formed her idea about humanity. Her vision of the person, male and female gives us an anthropology that sees humans, male and female as bearing the image of the Trinitarian God in their ability to create.

Sayers asks us to connect the behaviour of Christian theology and art and by doing so gain a clearer understanding of what a human being is. If we conclude, as she does, that "creative mind is the very grain of the

2. Sayers, "Vocation," 89.

3. Sayers, *Four Sacred Plays*, 103.

spiritual universe"[4] then it should be exhibited in the spiritual structure of every man and woman. This is her anthropology of human as creator which she immediately connects to daily life. She asks us if, by confining most people to uncreative activities and an uncreative outlook, we are doing violence to their very nature. The answer, for Sayers, is yes. This must have implications for education, employment, the war effort, economic and political life.

In this chapter I hope to show how her analogy of the Trinity and the anthropological description of humanity enriches Christian anthropology. I will then evaluate her extended study of her analogy, *The Mind of the Maker,* and examine her analogy against other Trinitarian theology. Finally, I compare Sayers' anthropology to MacIntyre's idea of a person, and the concept of human nature which lies at the centre of his ethics. I will show that Sayers' and MacIntyre's ideas on creativity as a dimension of the human being ground their discussions of work and human flourishing which are taken up in the following chapter.

Sayers understood herself to be writing an analogy that could help the ordinary person to see that the doctrine of the Trinity had relevance to life. She wasn't trying to extend the academic theology of the Trinity, nor was she claiming to give a comprehensive theological account of the Trinity.

Christian revelation was part of her mental background, and she can be categorized as a theologian who falls under the "faith seeking understanding" model which gives priority to revelation over experience. Therefore it is reasonable to see that having a mind formed in a Trinitarian faith, she would discover three-fold analogies; but she was also aware of, for example, the dichotomy of author and book or painter and audience, and the multiplicity of steps in creation, especially in the process of writing and editing text. Her own claims for the analogy are not that it proves the existence of the God as Trinity, but that she discovered a pattern, a three-ness, in her work as a writer. When she compared this pattern to the doctrine of the Trinity she found 'that between the two there is a difference only of technical phraseology . . . a difference, not of category, but only of quality and degree."[5]

Sayers' described some of her theological work as "disentangl[ing] the language-trouble by translating from one jargon to another."[6] In *The Mind*

---

4. Sayers, *Mind of the Maker,* 185.

5. Ibid., 182.

6. Sayers, *Letters Vol. 4,* 142.

of the Maker she was translating between the jargons of literary criticism and theology. She proposed this analogy to the Trinity to sort out the confusions of the multiple attacks on Christian dogma. She identified the incoherence in many of the charges made against the theology of the Trinity. If the critics say that the Trinity is simply an anthropomorphic projection by theologians, then they cannot the same time claim it is "apriorist and unrelated to human experience; since we are committed to supposing that is a plain *a posteriori* induction from human experience."[7] On the other hand, if critics claim that the doctrine is the product of revelation, pure religious experience from God interpreted by philosophy, then they cannot charge that it is irrational.

Readers are invited to investigate her account of creative mind and decide whether or not it is rational and fits with human experience. They can then evaluate the parallels Sayers drew between that experience and the Trinity and decide if it is a true analogy, an instance of the same pattern, as the behaviour of apples and planets are for gravity. Readers coming with her thus far have a further decision to make: does the pattern apply only to some people, those we identify as artists, or does that pattern apply to all human beings?[8] She would answer that it applies to all human beings and then draws out the implications for social ethics, particularly in regard to work. Thus, the criticism that she imposed a three-ness may be true, but does not invalidate her work. Readers are free to reject her analogy, and certainly free to reject belief in the Trinitarian God. If, however, they can understand her analogy, they may not claim that Christianity is irrational or unrelated to human experience.

Sayers' analogy: Idea, Energy and Power, is both a social and a psychological trinity. The analogy claims to describe the process any human creator experiences, but contains, in the third term, Power, the essential communion with others. Thus, the human creator is primarily relational. The analogy was exceptional for her day as being an individual, psychological analogy which had, of its essence, a social dimension. This social dimension is especially appropriate in an analogy for the Trinity in our age when current Trinitarian theology privileges social rather than psychological analogies. The purpose of drawing the analogy was also directed to the social: she wanted her audience to re-examine human work and revise their ideas about work and the economy.

7. Sayers, *Mind of the Maker*, 183.
8. Ibid., 185.

She put human creativity in dialogue with the idea of God's creating out of nothing and saw the problems any analogy would face: how can we understand the idea that God created out of nothing and how can we compare our creations to Creation? We do use the word create, as she writes, "to convey an extension and amplification of something that we do know. . . . If the word 'Maker' does not mean something related to our human experience of making, then it has no meaning at all. We extend it to the concept of a Maker who can make something out of nothing; we limit it to exclude the concept of employing material tools."[9]

The metaphor of creator has been less studied, she thinks for two reasons: first, Christ's sanction of the metaphor of God the Father, and secondly, our limited experience of the act of creation. We cannot create matter. We can, however, rearrange it. We acknowledge different kinds of creation from a machine which stamps out thousands of buttons as a poor and limited kind of creation to a piece of fashion known as a "creation" or a well-cooked steak which may be called a work of art.

In a poem or a painting, though, we see best matter mixed with thought that produces the new entity. And it is indeed a new entity: "The poet is not obliged, as it were, to destroy the material of a Hamlet in order to create a Falstaff."[10] Our physical experience of creating new beings is also part of our understanding of the concept of creation, as she says, "Outside our own experience of procreation and creation we can form no notion of how anything comes into being."[11]

Sayers had observed the three-fold structure of creating in herself, detailed the process in *Murder Must Advertise* and in the Archangel Michael's speech. She thinks this trinity is the natural consequence of humans bearing the image of a Trinitarian God, the Maker. She was aware of the doctrine's status. It "enjoys the greatest reputation for obscurity and remoteness from common experience."[12] St. Augustine used examples from life to explain three-in-oneness such as seeing: the form seen, the act of vision, and the mental attention which correlates the two. We can separate these three when we are thinking about seeing, but not when we are looking at the dog or an omelette chef in a top hat. Joseph Ratzinger thinks that Augustine's analogy of the Trinity to the person's mental acts is problematic, "As

9. Ibid., 27.
10. Ibid., 29.
11. Ibid., 30.
12. Ibid., 35.

a result, the Trinitarian concept of person was no longer transferred to the human person in all its immediate impact."[13]

Augustine's example of thought as a trinity of memory, understanding and will is instantly recognizable as a single thing of three aspects. So, Sayers claims, is a book for a writer: "If you were to ask the writer which is 'the real book'—his Idea of it, his Activity in writing it, or its return to himself in Power, he would be at a loss to tell you, because these things are essentially inseparable. Each of them is the complete book separately; yet in the complete book all of them exist together. He can, by an act of the intellect, 'distinguish the persons' but he cannot by any means 'divide the substance.'"[14]

And she says that based on this, our experience of a Trinitarian structure in our own process of creation, the Trinitarian structure of the Universe makes sense, and the doctrine of the Trinity is not something that is unrelated to us and our lives. In each of the examples, St. Augustine's and Sayers', we see that they have provided a three-some to be an analogy to the Trinity. Each choice for analogue could be described in two- or four-parts. So the analogies are not trying to prove the Trinity; they are trying to explain the Trinity. Sayers' is clearly not doing academic systematic theology, but practical theology giving the believer a starting point for approaching this central Christian doctrine.

When *The Mind of the Maker* appeared, it was received in religious and literary publications with mostly favourable reviews, although the review in *The Spectator* was dismissive of what it perceived as her egotism in using her own books and experience of writing them. The Roman Catholic reviewers in *The Tablet, The Dublin Review* and *Commonweal* thought that St Augustine's analogy Power to the Father, Idea to the Son, and Energy to Holy Ghost was more apt, but found her analogy interesting. Fr. Vann OP, writing in *Blackfriars,* was disappointed that the book as a whole did not work; in his view the connection between the analogy and the ethics of work was obscured by the chapters comparing literary creation of characters with human beings' free will and the author's obligation to the plot and the likelihood of miracles. The reviewer in the *Downside Review* was more enthusiastic and, with reservations about her failures to express her theology within the conventions of the Roman Catholic systematic theology

---

13. Ratzinger, "Concerning the Notion," 447.

14. Sayers, *Mind of the Maker*, 41.

of the day, recommended her social criticism as compatible with Roman Catholic Social Thought.

The analogy on which she bases her anthropology has two great strengths: first, it is a model of equality in diversity. Second, it is individual and social: the third person of this analogy, the Power, connects the creator and the audience. Sayers' analogy gives a theological basis to correct a Christian tradition that is sometimes misinterpreted to deny full humanity to women, such as Milton's "He for God only, she for God in him."[15]

Sayers sees creativity as a human power, common to men and women. Sayers' anthropology of a single human nature which is of its essence in communion with others, is an advance on the thinking which identifies men and women as so different as to have different natures, what is known in current theology as two-nature anthropology. By drawing out an analogy to the Trinity and basing her anthropology and therefore her social ethics on that analogy, Sayers provides a true theology of work. Work is not just a punishment for sin; it is an expression of our bearing the image of God. In her work the Trinity grounds a single-nature anthropology which can account for difference in equality.

The book *The Mind of the Maker* did not have a great impact on the Church of England, although it received some good reviews as detailed above. Thurmer points out three factors for its relatively small impact: "the date of publication, the author's fame as a detective novelist, and the prominence in the book of literary criticism."[16] In the same work he compares the work of other theologians to Sayers including Charles Raven and Karl Barth.[17] Thurmer quotes Charles Raven in *The Creator Spirit* (1928), who used the painter as a human analogy for the Trinity: "The artist's will which purposes to create the picture and the impulse which prepares pigments and canvas is God the Father . . . the artist's conception of the complete picture, his cartoon of the grand design . . . is God the Son . . . the artist's energy, the vital and creative activity whereby is produced upon the canvas of matter the perfect image which the will has planned and the vision conceived is God the Holy Spirit."[18]

15. Milton, *Paradise Lost,* Book IV, lines 296–98.

16. Thurmer, *Detection of the Trinity,* 59.

17. This study is directed to the implications for social ethics of Sayers' analogy of the Trinity. Therefore, the serious and extensive systematic work of theologians on the Trinity can only be touched on in an effort to show that Sayers' analogy was a plausible one, and one not dissimilar to those proposed by theologians of her day.

18. Thurmer, *Reluctant Evangelist,* 40.

This analogy like Augustine's relates Power to the Father, Idea to the Son and Energy to the Holy Spirit; but this fidelity to Augustine means it suffers as a description of creating an artwork. And, like Augustine's analogy, it leaves the work self-contained. Comparing it to Sayers' analogy Raven separates what Sayers calls the Energy, the Son, that is, the actual process of painting into two persons: the Father, the will and the preparation of the canvas and pigments, and the Spirit, the activity of painting. This means there is no term left for the reception of the work by the audience. Sayers' analogy, by making the Spirit analogous to her term the Power, the reception of the work by the lively soul, produces a sounder analogy because it is not only individual, it is social. The strength of Sayers' approach is shown in the anthropological implications of her analogy; the human is shown as essentially relational.

Rev. Leonard Hodgson commented on *The Mind of the Maker*, finding it interesting but suggesting that she may have confused the begetting of the Son with the creation of the world.[19] In correspondence with Sayers he notes that in his appendix about her book, "I am glad to see that after the quotation it goes on to interpret you rightly."[20] He suggests she alter the pages he commented on to make her meaning clearer if the book goes into a second edition. This suggests that he accepts her work as valid for its purpose.

Claude Welch treats Sayers' book as a serious work of theology and engages with it as such. He identifies a problem for Reformed theologians with analogy: "Miss Sayers accepts the Augustinian formulation in the Athanasian Creed as normative, and the psychological sort of analogy as obvious. . . . The basic difficulty which confronts all attempts to bring analogy to the defence of the doctrine of the Trinity is the question of what aspect of experience is to be chosen as the finite analogate. Unless we know already what the doctrine means, we have no way of determining which element of human experience can best serve as the basis for argument."[21]

Sayers could respond to this, I believe, by saying that she had experienced the process of creation and knew the doctrine of the Trinity. When she compared the two, she found that her experience illuminated the Creeds' statements.

19. Hodgson, *Doctrine of the Trinity*, 230.
20. Letters Sayers Wade MS 510/18.
21. Welch, *Trinity in Contemporary Theology*, 90.

Systematic theology about the Trinity has seen a great revival in the past twenty years in Christian theological circles. Christopher Schwöbel writes that the pressure for a revived and renewed Trinitarian theology has come from the ecumenical dialogue between Western Christian theologians and the Orthodox theologians and from the challenge of atheism to Christianity.[22] Theologians are seriously considering Karl Rahner's ideas that most Christians are almost monotheists and that "should the doctrine of the Trinity have to be dropped as false, the major part of religious literature could well remain unchanged."[23] Catherine Mowry LaCugna's study, *God for Us: the Trinity and Christian Life* was written in response to Rahner's observations to reconnect the Trinity with theology, ethics, spirituality and the life of the Church.[24]

Most of the new systematic work is outside the scope of this study, focussing as it does on the philosophical background of the doctrine and the reinterpretation of theological language, and the status of the doctrine within an understanding of the possibilities of revelation and reception of the canonical texts. This study, in contrast, is centered on the renewed theological anthropology. It must be said that with the exception of Mascall, none of the modern studies have mentioned Sayers' work in this area, so we must say that her work may be regarded as a lost prophecy of things to come rather than a signpost on the way. To place Sayers' work within current Trinitarian theology, I will look at the possibility of analogies to the Trinity and their characteristics, and the anthropology which results from a renewed Trinitarianism. Finally, I will compare Sayers' work to current work which examines artists and creativity in relation to the Trinity.

Brown, as one would expect from a philosophical theologian, states clearly that "no satisfactory analogy can be provided for what is ultimately a unity being also fundamentally a plurality or for what is fundamentally a plurality being ultimately a unity."[25] He notes that unsatisfactory as analogies may be, without analogies, doubts are bound to be increased.[26] In a

---

22. A selection of current work illustrates the great interest in the topic: Hill, *Three-personed God* (1982); Brown, *Divine Trinity* (1985); Schwöbel and Gunton, *Persons Divine and Human* (1991); Gunton, *One, the Three and the Many* (1993); J. Thompson, *Modern Trinitarian Perspectives* (1994); Schwöbel, *Trinitarian Theology Today: Essays on Divine Being and Act* (1995); and Davis et al., *Trinity: An Interdisciplinary Symposium on the Trinity* (1999).

23. Rahner, *Trinity*, 10–11.

24. LaCugna, *God for Us*, ix.

25. Brown, *Divine Trinity*, 12.

26. Ibid., 275.

later essay on the Trinity in art, he writes that the artist's intention is "less the doctrine as such or the raison d'etre of its unity and much more it relevance to us."[27]

Schwöbel talks of constructing new models of the Trinity, psychological or social; but sees that in the current climate the social models seem to be preferred.[28] He allows both approaches, from human to divine personhood and from divine to human personhood since persons are in the image of God and are destined eschatologically "to participate through the Spirit in the personal relationship of the Son to the Father."[29] La Cugna noted that the analogy of God to the soul, found in Augustine, is usually presented as is "God and the soul alike . . . are both self-enclosed, self-related."[30] It is this enclosure, and the radical individualism it seems to create that is rejected by contemporary theologians.

The concept of the person in modernity is problematic. Human beings are seen as an economic or commercial cipher, a memory with no intentions, a mind-body problem, or an ahistoric abstraction. In German idealism and British utilitarianism: "essentially, human beings are viewed as moral and/or methodological constructs; the person is a heuristic device with no guts or history, and in its non-Kantian forms, no self-consciousness either. . . . Much of early existentialism trapped humankind on a private island of self-authentication cut off from the mainland of history and tradition."[31]

This concept of the person is rejected by Anglican, Reformed, Roman Catholic and Orthodox theologians. So for example, Mascall, an Anglican, quotes Galot, a Roman Catholic: "The mystery of the Trinity is presented as the sharpest denial of any individualistic personalism."[32] The British Council of Churches' report titled *The Forgotten Trinity* states: "By concentrating on reason or freedom or our moral sense as the basis of our distinctive humanity, the tradition has been frequently tempted into an individualistic, or indeed, merely a secular anthropology: the image of God is that which human beings individually possess."[33] Gunton, of the Reformed tradition,

---

27. Brown, "Trinity in Art," 349.

28. Schwöbel, *Trinitarian Theology Today*, 1.

29. LaCugna, *God for Us*, 13.

30. Ibid., 103.

31. British Council of Churches, *Forgotten Trinity*, 139–40.

32. Mascall, *Triune God*, 29.

33. British Council of Churches, *Forgotten Trinity*, 23.

wrote in *The One, the Three and the Many*, "Human being in the image of God is to be understood relationally rather than in terms of the possession of fixed characteristics such as reason or will."[34] Zizioulas, an Orthodox theologian writes: "The Cappadocian Fathers gave to the world the most precious concept it possesses: *the concept of the person, as an ontological concept in the ultimate sense* . . . true personhood arises not from one's individualistic isolation from others but from love and relationship with others, from communion."[35] The ecumenical exchanges have borne fruit as the insights of the Cappadocian fathers are enriching all streams of the renewed Trinitarian theology. LaCugna writes: "Trinitarian theology could be described as par excellence a theology of relationship, which explored the mysteries of love, relationship, personhood and communion within the framework of God's self-revelation in the person of Christ and the activity of the Spirit."[36]

The person is in relation not only to other persons but the non-personal world; human destiny is found in human community and human responsibility to the universe. Dulles makes a similar point: "To be human is to be socially and historically constituted."[37] Equally, to be human is to create social ties and a history, a narrative in MacIntyre's words: "[t]he narrative of any one life is part of an interlocking set of narratives . . . its unity is the unity of a narrative embodied in a single life."[38] Here the theology of the Trinity and human creativity meet. The Orthodox theologian Ziziou-lous presents it clearly: "he, unlike the animals, is not satisfied with the given being and wishes to affirm freely identities of his own, thus creating his own world (e.g. in art, in unconditional love, in forgiveness)."[39]

Gunton agrees "The distinctive feature of created persons is their mediating function in the achievement of perfection by the rest of creation. They are called to be the forms of action, in science, ethics and art—in a word, to culture—which enable to take place the sacrifice of praise which is the free offering of all things, perfected, to their creator."[40]

34. Gunton, *One, The Three*, 5.

35. Zizioulas, "On Being a Person," 56–59.

36. LaCugna, *God for Us*, 1.

37. Dulles, *Craft of Theology*, 20.

38. MacIntyre, *After Virtue*, 218.

39. Zizioulas, "On Being a Person," 44.

40. Gunton, *One, The Three*, 230.

Brian Horne in his article "Art: A Trinitarian Imperative?" sees creativity as essential to being human. He never mentions Sayers, but by looking at the experience of creating arrives at a place that echoes her own understanding of creativity. He finds that the activity of the imagination bringing into being a new work of art makes the individual feel "god-like." He characterises the drive to create as a compulsion to embody in material form the visions of the inner eye. He writes: "while the argument for the possibility or potentiality, of artistic creation is lodged in the doctrine of the image (creation); the propriety of artistic creation is lodged in the doctrine of the Incarnation; and the necessity or inevitability of artistic creation is lodged in the doctrine of the Spirit."[41]

The three-fold process of moving out from the self in order to find the self, the compulsion for self-expression and self-knowledge is the basis of all art. His work supports the contention of this study that Sayers has a valid insight into creativity as a human analogue which can help us to understand the Trinitarian revelation of God. Unlike Sayers, he does not make this process something that every human should experience, how each human should live a fully human life.

In a theology about relationality, for what else but relation constitutes the Trinity for Augustine, the current work highlights the radical equality of the Trinity. This in turn has, in some ways, surprising results for religious language, and tremendous implications for social ethics. LaCugna sees the new understanding of the doctrine of the Trinity with precedence of person over substance as having the implication in all of politics and ethics of a primacy of equality over hierarchy.[42] Francis Martin criticises LaCugna for her thesis that in actual fact we can know nothing of the internal relations of the Trinity but only their economic or enacted relations.[43] I believe he has misinterpreted her understanding of what the economic Trinity does reveal, and further, that his criticism, even if valid, does not weaken her arguments for putting the Trinity in its richness into a renewal of the liturgical, sacramental, and moral life of the Christian community. Dulles calls the Trinity the deepest mystery of communication, "a totally free and complete sharing among equals."[44] LaCugna calls us to make Christian orthopraxis correspond to what we believe about God: "that God is personal, that God

---

41. Horne, "Art," 90.

42. LaCugna, *God for Us*, 399.

43. Martin, *Feminist Question*, 285–87.

44. Dulles, *Craft of Theology*, 37.

is ecstatic and fecund love, that God's very nature is to exist toward and for another. . . . The reign of God is governance for the sake of communion. It entails a radical reordering of existence: our attachments, our familial relationships, our worship, our fears and anxieties, our ways of relating to others."[45]

Mascall notes that the Incarnation is another pointer to equality; it shows us that total dependence does not necessarily involve inferiority.[46] Current Trinitarian theology gives us a theological anthropology of equals who relate not in relations of domination but of true communion.[47]

In this theology sexuality is not ignored or set aside as a problem for moral theologians, not fit for consideration in the higher reaches of systematic theology: "Sexuality broadly defined is the capacity for relationship, for ecstasies, for self-transcendence. Sexuality lies at the heart of all creation and is an icon of who God is, the God in whose image we were created male and female. Sexuality is a clue that our existence is grounded in a being whose To-Be is To-Be-For."[48]

This has a direct bearing on the family in social ethics, on gender roles in care-giving and on the meaning of equality in the family, discussed more fully in chapter 5. Trinitarian theology with the vision of communion not domination gives a new vision for political life as well. This theology serves as a critical observer of cultural life, and condemns that which reduces persons to instruments or cogs in a machine. A theological anthropology of person as relational, and a conception of the people of God as an egalitarian communion of persons rather than a hierarchy of superiors and inferiors is a sound basis for a social ethic.

Clearly theologians concerned with saying something meaningful about social ethics, sexual ethics, sacramental theology, or ecclesiology have had to rethink, or at least make explicit their concept of a person and the concept of gender. In dogmatic theology, the definition of Christ as having a human and a divine nature presumes that you know what a human nature is. The Trinity is one God of three persons: if the dogma has any meaning, the theologians must have a concept of person. O'Neill gives a general definition of theological anthropology and its sources: "Theological anthropology, itself a relatively new member of the family of theological concerns,

---

45. LaCugna, *God for Us*, 383–84.

46. Mascall, *Triune God*, 32–33.

47. LaCugna, *God for Us*, 399.

48. Ibid., 407.

raises and answers the question "What does our faith teach us about the mystery of being human?" While every faith tradition has an implicit or explicit theological anthropology, what distinguishes Christian anthropology is that it answers the question on the basis of Christian revelation and on the experience of life in the Christian community of believers."[49]

This adds the distinctive dimension of communion. This is a sign of the movement away from the person understood as autonomous individual, the conception of modernity, to person as person in communion which is being recovered in current theological anthropology. It is against this enlarged understanding of the person that Sayers' anthropology will be examined.

Sayers' Anthropology

Begin Here (1939) highlights several key parts of Sayers' anthropology, first of all, the high value she places on the individual: "Before going further I want to make it quite clear that when I say "Man", I mean, not a generalised figure representing the Human Race, but the individual man. I mean you. I mean me. I mean your grocer, Mr. Brown, and my charwoman, Mrs. Smith."[50]

She restates her central understanding of human nature:

> To be merely passive, merely receptive, is a denial of human nature. "God", says the author of Genesis, "created man in His own image"; and of the original of that image he tells us one thing only: "In the beginning, God created". That tells us plainly enough what the writer thought about the essential nature of man.
>
> It is because of this that, in a mechanised civilisation like ours, the average man and woman find themselves—despite a multitude of comforts and conveniences—unhappy, at a loss, and disoriented. . . . What they chiefly miss is the power and opportunity to be actively creative.[51]

Sayers' novels and plays, especially her handling of the Peter Wimsey–Harriet Vane romance and her essays "Are Women Human?" and "The Human-Not-Quite-Human" comprise a disavowal of a two-nature

---

49. O'Neill, "Mystery of Being Human," 140.

50. Sayers, *Begin Here*, 29.

51. Ibid., 23.

anthropology. Both essays and fiction are still read and quoted with approval by feminist writers today.[52]

Sayers was not an active participant in the women's movement of her day, and was hesitant, as others were, of claiming the label "feminist." However, when the opportunity occurred she was prepared to make the case for her view that women should be regarded as human. Today we would characterise her position as an anthropology of a single human nature expressed in two genders. Her goal was having women recognised as human beings first and as female second. This is precisely what makes Sayers of interest to many theologians today. Ann Loades writes: "What makes the writings of Dorothy L. Sayers of contemporary interest is the way in which she more often than not argued for the importance of the contribution of women by insisting on the irrelevance of such sexual difference to the particular issue in question."[53]

Sayers recognised that biology played a part in making individuals who they were, but she never viewed it as totally determinative. She recognised that the variations between individuals, whether biological, psychological, cultural or any other, were as significant as the similarities between them were. She wanted men and women to be free to do work that suited each individual's talents. Her central claim was that men and women are human beings first and only secondarily feminine or masculine. This, of course, directly confronts the anthropology which defines women by their sexual/reproductive function and subordinates all questions, whether of women's work, education or their social role, to the responsibility to fulfil the mother's role.

Sayers rarely quoted Scripture in her writing, nevertheless we can see that "In the image of God he created them, male and female he created them" (Gen. 1:27) and "there is no longer male and female" (Gal. 3:28) are the starting assumptions in her writings. We can see the development of her thought not only in *Begin Here*, but also in her notes, "What is Man?" where she examines various philosophies' and religions' attempts to explain man, understood by her to mean, as throughout her writings, men and women.[54]

---

52. See, for example, O'Neill, "Mystery of Being Human Together," Haack, "After My Own Heart," and Loades, *Feminist Theology Voices*.

53. Loades, *Feminist Theology Voices*, 2.

54. Sayers, "What Is Man?"

She distinguishes two kinds of explanation: those offered by Platonism or the major religions which explain the lower in terms of the higher, and those offered by materialism which explain the higher in terms of the lower.

The first type of explanation accounts for the disjunction in humankind by, in the case of Christianity, the Fall. The second type of explanation says that the evil humans experience belongs to a) inorganic elements, b) animal ancestry or c) delusions. This, she maintains, cannot explain why we have a sense of guilt, and means that we "only got rid of the doctrine of *original sinfulness* [emphasis in original] to get in its place the far more desperate doctrine of *individual guilt* [emphasis in original]."[55] She had expressed the same thought in "Creed or Chaos?" "The delusion of the mechanical perfectibility of mankind through a combined process of scientific knowledge and unconscious evolution has been responsible for a great deal of heartbreak;"[56] and in "The Church in the New Age": "The primary delusion of the enlightened pagan is an incurable optimism about human nature. He is persuaded that there is nothing intrinsically wrong with man, and that if only his exterior circumstances could be satisfactorily adjusted he would settle down in peace and security to be as good and happy as the day is long."[57]

The second type of explanation also means that paradise is not in the past, nor in the present, but in some future point of history and it is not a paradise for the individual, but for humanity as a race. This she found outrageous: "Our good sense and our decency are sufficiently outraged by the idea that a million labouring John Smiths should be exploited and sacrificed for the benefit of a few rich John Smiths; but what is this beside the monstrous injustice which would sacrifice and exploit the whole past and present for the sake of the happy and prosperous John Smiths to be born at the end of history?"[58]

She wrote of the "Church's doctrine of man" as giving us an explanation for what man is, why he is not perfectible, and what the purpose of human life is.[59] A human being obeys the laws of the natural universe and the animal kingdom. Nevertheless, she maintained that there is "an immense

---

55. Sayers, *Making Sense of the Universe*, 8.
56. Sayers, *Creed or Chaos?* 40.
57. Sayers, "Church in New Age," 12.
58. Sayers, *Making Sense of the Universe*, 10.
59. Sayers, "What is Man?" 9.

difference between him and the most elaborate of animals."[60] Humans are formed in the image of a superior being with awareness toward, and a responsibility to, that being. The Fall means that human nature is twisted out of truth, and the best qualities in a person became corrupted, and all our truths became heresies in her definition, the "insistence on one truth to the neglect of the opposing truth."[61] Hence, our best qualities, now deified and self-directed by the fall, are corrupted. She gives these examples in the document laid out as shown below:

[best qualities]	[deified]	[resulting corruption]
Love	possessiveness	morbidity, promiscuity, divorce
Family	oppression	break up and rebellion
Knowledge	relativity	negation
Peace	toleration	war
Freedom	competition	total tyranny[62]

In her speeches and writings during the war years and immediately afterwards, she returned again and again to the Church's doctrine of fallen humanity as a sign of hope.

Sayers one-nature anthropology now needs defence from those called "difference feminists" such as Carol Gilligan. Sayers was defending, in the words of contemporary feminist Susan Haack:

> two main positive themes: that women are fully human beings, just as men are; and that, like all human beings, women are individuals, each one different. . . . Doubtless some will see Sayers's whole approach as passé, a holdover from the Dark Ages before Second Wave feminism; but I see it as a much needed antidote to the emphasis on women-as-a-class which predominates feminism today. . . . How much better it would be if, instead of casting around for an epistemology that represents, "the feminist point of view" we tried, as feminists, finally to get beyond the stereotypes and as epistemologists, to develop a true account of knowledge, evidence, warrant, inquiry, etc. Then we might be readier to acknowledge that any halfway adequate epistemology will need to be at once quasi-logical, personal, and social; concerned with the

60. Ibid., 10.

61. Ibid., 11.

62. Ibid.

cognitive capacities and limitations that all human beings share, and with the idiosyncrasies, expertise and imaginative contributions of individuals; looking to the way interactions among individuals may compensate for this individual's perceptual and intellectual defects, while keeping the insights only that individual could contribute.[63]

Sayers saw that the two-nature anthropology was inadequate for men and for women; she proposed instead a single anthropology for the human being based on humanity bearing the image of God the Creator in the human ability to create. The central feature of her anthropology is its emphasis on human creativity. In "Vocation in Work", she wrote of an affinity between the Christian value on creativity with part of Marxist anthropology: "And here we may look at what the materialist dogma of communism has said about man's nature: 'Man is first man when he produces the means of livelihood.' The means of livelihood. To the assertion 'Man is only man when he produces (or makes),' the Christian may readily assent."[64]

This creativity was the heart of Sayers' anthropology. In the same article she wrote: "And then He made man 'in his own image'—a creature in the image of a Creator. . . . he [man] makes things—not just one uniform set of necessary things, as a bee makes a honey-comb, but an interminable variety of different and no strictly necessary things, because he wants to. . . . Even in this fallen and unsatisfactory life, man is still so near His divine pattern that he continually makes things, as God makes things, for the fun of it. He is *homo faber*—man the craftsman.[65]

Her theological anthropology posits that every person bears the image of God in the ability to create. The process of creation as she described it is relational in the third term, the Power, and therefore Sayers' anthropology is also relational. Each person exists in relation to others; no individual is isolated, each creator creates with materials supplied by the Creator, and presents work to other creatures. She did not develop the theme of relationality when she was writing *The Mind of the Maker*: the experience of the war had made one's responsibility to the community and the experience of being part of that community the very atmosphere to everyday life. Secondly, as a Christian, she saw each human as part of Christ's mystical body, but

---

63. Haack, "After My Own heart."

64. Sayers, "Vocation," 90.

65. Ibid., 89.

did not explicitly draw out the implications of that until her play, *The Just Vengeance* (1946).

A critic may charge that creativity is not an essential part of humanity, and that Sayers' use of "create" and "make" fuse two very different terms: the person cooking a meal is "making" but not "creating" in the same sense that the artist is creating when making a poem or a painting. Secondly, the critic may say that there is no necessary relationality in her analogy: an artist can create a painting and refuse to show it to anyone.

In answer to the first, Sayers was writing within the Christian tradition and its idea of the creature endowed with freedom. She does not explore exactly how that idea and the idea that we bear the image of the Creator in our own ability to create are mutually dependent. All human creativity is a limited creativity, dependent on God's creation. However, it is a real creativity; the cooked meal is a new thing, and represents one of several possibilities given any set of raw ingredients. To limit creativity to the artist does not recognize the effect each person has on the material world, for good or ill. In answer to the second, it is true that the artist can refuse to share his work of art, or even to embody it in paint or words; however, the expression of the artist through his or her medium is generally meant to be shared. Since this is our common experience, we can understand her third term of Power, and see the relationality at the heart of this analogue.

The artist, in any event, is a person. We need an account of persons that includes childhood, old age, disability, and dependency—the universal experience of humans which establishes relationality as a biological necessity. Sayers has not given us this account, but MacIntyre has in *Dependent Rational Animals*. He develops his argument that to become independent practical reasoners: "the acquisition of the necessary virtues, skills, and self-knowledge is something that we in key part owe to those particular others on whom we have to depend."[66] Even when we are independent, we need others to sustain us. We are never the autonomous individual, separated from other human beings, that is pictured in modern moral philosophy. This account of the interconnectedness of human life yields an ethical anthropology of relationality. This can remain on the natural level, rather than the theological level, but it equally defines what it is "to be" human as "to be for" relationship.

---

66. MacIntyre, *Dependent*, 96.

MacIntyre and Sayers read together produce an anthropology of the human which values the biological realities, sees persons as relational, and essentially creative. The foundation for Sayers' claims about work is solid.

Sayers' concentrating on work and human creativity (rather than human procreativity) in her analogy highlights the anthropology of humanity as creators. Thurmer says that this image was regarded with suspicion. He identifies two strands to that suspicion: the fear of idolatry in the Bible, where "the work of men's hands" is often actually an idol; and the Greek classical tradition with the warnings against pride, particularly pride in craftsmen.[67] Sayers was not alone in finding a trinity in the creative process. Tischler identifies Sayers' *idea* with Abram's *author* and Aquinas's *integrity* or *unity*; her *energy* with Abram's *artefact* and Aquinas' *proportion* and her *power* with Abram's *audience* and Aquinas' *splendour.* However, Aquinas' trinity is a trinity by which aesthetic work is judged. Abram's three terms seem to be more about the process of creativity and parallel Sayers' three terms.[68]

It is apparent that many artists never look beyond themselves for an external archetype. Sayers, herself a committed Christian, does do so, and perhaps other Christian artists also do so. Her experience as a playwright which she recounted gives us an insight into a real experience of creativeness that seems to approach the divine in a way that more ordinary experiences of creativity, making a cake or a sculpture, do not. The author's words create a new world populated by new characters with narratives and lives that are complete but only partially revealed. Her own experiences grappling with the Gospels to produce the radio plays influenced her anthropology and her speeches on work through the period. Given the unpredictability in human life, and the doctrine of humans as bearing the image of God, Sayers was right to say that all human beings are creative; it is not a special gift reserved for the artists.

In Sayers' discussion of her analogy and claim that we bear the image of God in our ability to create she does not bring out that the primary way we bear the image of God is in our capacity for God.[69] This is the dynamic experience of each human; seeking God expresses the image, turning from God disfigures the image. Given this traditional understanding of image of God, Sayers' analogy actually strengthens and makes more understand-

---

67. Thurmer, *Detection of the Trinity*, 51.

68. Tischler, "Artist," 162–63.

69. Augustine, *De Trinitate* XIV, 8, 11.

able Augustine's conception of how humans bear the image of a Trinitarian God. The Idea, the end in the beginning, is the life-long search for God; the Energy, the working out of the Idea, is life on earth in its difficulties and limitations; the Power, the response, is in the bond within the Body of Christ, the Church, in communion with humanity and God.

Sayers' analogy gives new insights into the Trinity, though it is limited as any analogy must be, and it yields an ethic of work which offers a critique of the economy based on a theologically sophisticated anthropology which is congruent with our current theological anthropologies. MacIntyre's contribution, identifying the poverty of the conceptions of humanity in analytic philosophy and existentialism and situating the person in relation to the community, fills out Sayers' anthropology. Together they uncover resources within the natural law tradition to develop a theology and ethic of work which properly values the work of care and the practice of the family in a gender neutral way. This will be taken up in the next chapter.

5

Good Work

> If man's fulfilment of his nature is to be found in the full expression
> of his divine creativeness, then we urgently need a Christian doc-
> trine of work, which shall provide, not only for proper conditions
> of employment, but also that the work shall be such as a man may
> do with his whole heart, and that he shall do it for the very work's
> sake.[1]

IN THE CHRISTIAN TRADITION work has always had two meanings: it is a
stewardship of God's creation (Gen 1:28) and a punishment for sin (Gen
3:19). Work is toil, a discipline for mastering the passions and a social duty.
The rise of industry created three new and related problems for a theology
of work: gender separation, the separation of secular work from Christian
vocation, and the conditions of work on an industrial assembly line.
Although in the developed world, some attempts at solving these problems
have been made, Sayers' theology and ethics of work are still relevant.

The gender separation was marked by the glorification of the woman
in the home. Sayers wrote: "The boast 'My wife doesn't need to soil her
hands with work,' first became general when the commercial middle classes
acquired the plutocratic and aristocratic notion that the keeping of an idle
woman was a badge of superior social status. Man must work, and woman
must exploit his labour. What else are they there for? And if the woman

---

1. Sayers, *Creed*, 45.

submits, she can be cursed for her exploitation; and if she rebels, she can be cursed for competing with the male."[2]

Sayers pointed out that most of the creative work of brewing, baking, and textile making had been removed from the home. Sayers, like other writers of her day, claimed that women needed meaningful occupation as well as satisfying emotional outlets and that the home no longer provided these.

The second problem was the division between secular work and religion. This divides the laity who work from the priests and religious who have a vocation. For Sayers, this division arose both from the Church's refusal to acknowledge the autonomy of the secular vocation and from the laity's identification of the church with the clergy.[3] A theology of work must be a theology based on Christian, Trinitarian anthropology that recognises the equality of men and women and a theology based on the universal call to holiness that empowers the laity to live their Christian vocation in their secular work. Sayers' writings on work meet both of these standards.

The third problem was the inhuman conditions of the work available within the factories of the industrial age. Labor in the household and the fields is hard toil, but it is part of a larger cycle of life and a local community within which the worker can see the result of his labour. On the assembly line of classic Taylorism, workers do a single task repetitively and never see the finished product of their work. They have no control over what is made, how it is made, or the speed at which it is made. Marx correctly diagnosed workers in the industrial economy as alienated from their work.

From the perspective of someone living in the 1920s and 1930s, it seemed that they were living through the last throes of capitalism with sustained unemployment even through what economists termed a recovery. Capitalism was not providing work for most workers, or a minimum standard of living or security to most potential workers. Much of the work that was available was work of the most inhuman kind in the factory. Peter Drucker in *The End of Economic Man*, which Sayers read and which forms one of the two main streams of inspiration for her work *Begin Here*, claimed that people no longer believed in economic man, in either the capitalist or the communist version, and that this collapse of belief in progress through industrialisation was the basis for the rise of the fascist totalitarian regimes. In the ferment of discussion inside and outside the churches several major

2. Sayers, *Unpopular Opinions*, 120.

3. Sayers, "Church's Responsibility," 71.

proposals to resolve this situation appeared. The Marxists developed the ideology of work within the communist revolution. Within the churches some recommended changing who owns the means of production; others wanted to adjust the existing economic system by creating unions to improve the wages and conditions of labour including a family wage or payment to women in the home for their work. The Distributivists and the *Christendom* group advocated a return to a pre-industrial, small-scale society.

The papal encyclicals *Rerum Novarum* and *Quadragesimo Anno* opposed the exploitation of the workers, and supported their rights to organize into unions and to a family wage. The encyclicals supported a limited right to private property and explained the dangers of unrestricted capitalism and of a purely materialistic socialism. The two encyclicals, in the face of what seemed to be the collapse of capitalism, demanded that any changes to the economic and political system recognize the theological dimension of man. *Quadragesimo Anno* states, "Just as the unity of human society cannot be founded on an opposition of classes, so also the right ordering of economic life cannot be left to the free competition of forces."[4] The major questions within the Anglican Social ethics debate of the period were unemployment and ownership of the means of production. Sayers was a prophetic voice in Christian social ethics of her day because her approach to the problem of work in the industrial economy was an anthropological one. Based on her analogy of the Trinity to the process of artistic creation, she proposed the artist as the model for all workers, male and female. Work to suit human beings must be work that allows them to exercise their creativity, and work as an artist works. This standard for evaluating work is basic. Starting with this understanding, the workplace can be transformed whether that workplace exists in a socialist, communist, or capitalist society.

Alasdair MacIntyre's philosophy, put in dialogue with Sayers, expands the account to include the work of care. He does not write directly about work, but in his *After Virtue* project, he critiques modern individualism and liberal capitalism. MacIntyre accepted as correct Marx's analysis of the worker as losing his humanity when his labour was turned into a commodity. One unchanging feature of MacIntyre's philosophical life has been his view of the destructive character of the institutions of capitalism, including the modern bureaucratic state.[5] MacIntyre contrasts those institutions

---

4. Pope Pius XII, *Quadragesimo Anno*, 88.

5. Murphy, *Alasdair MacIntyre*, 3.

with practices, human activities within a community through which one becomes virtuous.

Sayers' idea of good work has two parts: it must be work that makes a good product and be work that done in a humane process. The question of a good product is a question of value that Sayers' account does not completely answer. MacIntyre's idea of the practice as a school of the virtues fills out her account of the worker capable of making responsible choices about what work to do and what products to buy. Sayers' idea of a humane process as essential to good work is confirmed by modern literature on job design. Sayers opposed the separate spheres of work for men and women and proposed instead a standard that the job should be done by the person who does it best whether man or woman. Since she was writing against the gender stereotypes which limited women to the work of care, she did not defend that as good work. MacIntyre's account of the virtues of acknowledged dependence gives an account of the family and household that is free of gender stereotyping. MacIntyre's criticism of the institutions that support practices, and the institutions of global capitalism complete Sayers' criticisms of bureaucracy.

Sayers' Ideal Worker, the Artist

Sayers' writings centred on the idea of integrity in work, and work as essential to a good human life. All her speeches and writing about work were based on a sacramental understanding of creation, and her anthropology of the human as bearing the image of God in the ability to create.[6] The doctrine of the Fall meant work was seen as punishment for sin and would now be attended with difficulties, but not that work itself was a punishment. Sayers distinguishes work for the sake of the task from work for a livelihood, and identifies the latter with the punishment of sin.[7] This punishment is redeemed by Christ and our work must be redemptive as well: human situations are subject to the law of human nature, whose evil is at all times rooted in its good, and whose good can only redeem, but not abolish, its evil.[8]

As she contrasted respectability and virtue in her novels, she contrasts the creative worker with the industrious apprentice who was sober, thrifty,

6. Sayers, "Vocation in Work," 89. See also "Christ the Worker" in Appendix II.

7. Sayers, "Do Writers Work?" 4.

8. Sayers, *Mind of the Maker*, 191.

clean and respectable, but who did not question the work he did or its conditions. If work is viewed solely as a discipline, or the punishment for sin,
Sayers' question, "what work is fit for humans?" makes no sense, because
any and all work will serve this purpose, and indeed drudgery and mo-
notony would be expected.

Sayers expected responsible people to question what work they are
asked to do, how they are asked to do that work, and what effects their work
has on the community. These questions existed whatever the economic and
political system. She saw the Church as able to offer a critique of any system. A right understanding of work respects the two sources of real value
in the world: human labor and nature. We are not conquerors of creation,
"we ought not to treat Nature as the Germans treat a conquered province,
by spoiling, ravaging and destroying for our own greed."[9]

All humans are called to live creatively, whatever their work. Sayers
proposes that the artist is the model for the good life, not, certainly, because
of artists' morals, as conventionally understood, nor because she thought
artists had a superior, special, contemplative perception of life. It was precisely because artists create, even though most artists would not theologise
about their experiences as Sayers had done.

Her ideas differ from some of her contemporaries who wrote about
work and art in that she did not automatically value the hand made over
the machine made. Etienne Borne and François Henry in *A Philosophy of
Work* rejected the idea of work defined as a creative act. Art is work, but
not all work is art. They see an art work as having something not just the
artist's best efforts, but "something or other indefinite which trembles at the
delicate point of his soul which is worth more than all the success of intelligence and will."[10] Eric Gill in *Work and Leisure* had a wide definition of art:
"Art is the whole business of human making, the whole activity of man in
every department of life, seen in itself as a thing and not simply as a means
to an end, is the thing called art."[11] However, he, like Borne and Henry, sees
the human maker as adding an essential dimension to a finished object:
"Just because industrial products, however useful and however beautiful,
have not the tenderness of human works, they remain unsatisfying."[12]

9. Sayers, "Christ the Worker," 2.
10. Borne, *Philosophy of Work*, 127.
11. Gill, *Work and Leisure*, 15.
12. Ibid., 43.

Sayers' definition of the creative recognised both the differences and similarities between the artist's experience of creativity and that of the dressmaker or the cook: the human mind engaging with material to produce a thing, whether a loaf of bread, a dress, or a painting. All human beings have this capacity, while clearly all human beings do not have the capacity to be great painters, sculptors, writers, or artists as we usually understand that word. And all human beings have the capacity to work, as the artist does, in tune with human nature.

This demands a reorientation of each individual's view of life. She defined what she meant by "living creatively" in *The Mind of the Maker*. She distinguished two ways of living. The first, the positivistic, scientific approach, looks at life as a series of problems to be solved. Our job is then to find the solution and apply it. The artist, however, lives outside this problem/solution paradigm. To the artist, life presents a series of opportunities to make something new.

She described the experience of those who live in the problem/solution mode: the more problems they solve, the more problems they create, only now larger and more complex. The artist takes a different, a creative approach to life. She wrote, "The concept of 'problem and solution' is as meaningless, as applied to the act of creation as it is when applied to the act of pro-creation."[13] We must not "solve" our problems but "make something of them." She gave the rose as an example. She asked, "how will you proceed to solve a rose?"[14] The flower arranger, the gardener, the painter, and the perfumers were occupied with the rose itself, respecting its integrity, living creatively. This she compared to the geneticist solving the problem of producing a blue rose, or the chemist finding the chemical composition of the rose.

When the problem of a difficult site is solved with a well-designed building, it appears to the observer as the solution. Yet to Sayers that is a misunderstanding of the open-ended nature of the creative process. Many buildings would suit the site depending on the architect's vision and competence. The artist is not seeking the one correct answer; the artist is creating his own new thing out of the materials in the situation. The essential difference between problem solving and creating is whether or not the mind works with freedom.

13. Sayers, *Mind of the Maker*, 186–87.
14. Ibid., 209–10.

To clarify what change in attitude she proposed, she described four characteristics which distinguish problems capable of solution such as those in mathematics or in a piece of detective fiction, from the experiences of life which demand the creative approach. First, the detective problem is always soluble since it is constructed to be solved. In life there is no solution to the most pressing and universal problem, death. Sayers points out two things we can do with death: postpone it, or transfer the whole set of values connected with death to another sphere, eternity.[15] Second, the detective problem is completely soluble. In life, though, we are faced with problems which arise from our desire to enjoy contradictory things, freedom and order, or liberty and equality. In such cases there cannot be a solution but only attempts to construct a satisfactory balance between them. Any solution we reach may bring the intended consequence of a particular problem solved, but is certain to produce unpredictable, unintended consequences, the source of new problems.

Third, "The detective problem is solved in the same terms it is set."[16] This is possibly the greatest difference between the creative approach to life and to problem/solution approach. The artist crosses boundaries, refusing to be limited to the terms of the problem. Sayers describes the artist as laying his hand on the major premise, the universal statement which others leave unquestioned, and thus rocking the world. She herself is a good example of this; she refused to accept the premises of the argument about unemployment within the existing economic system. She questions the entire system.

Her final characteristic of the problem/solution mentality is "The detective problem is finite."[17] No artist accepts his work as finished. Each work of art however complete in itself it may appear to others, inspires the artist to a new work to express what is missing in the finished piece. No work can be perfect, or complete. Each is an opportunity for a new creative effort. In the same way, life presents us with situations which demand we make something new, and whatever we make will be imperfect, incomplete, and call us to further efforts.

She distinguished two groups of people: those who look upon work as a hateful necessity and those who look upon their work as an opportunity

15. Ibid., 197.

16. Ibid., 202.

17. Ibid., 204.

for enjoyment and self-fulfilment;[18] those who work to make money so that they can escape work, as compared to those who make money so that they may go on working. If the Christian understanding of work as the natural exercise and function of man, creative activity undertaken for the love of the work itself[19] and a full expression of worker's faculties, work should be not primarily a thing one does to live, but the thing one lives to do.[20]

The group who works for a livelihood, that is, works in order to escape work, includes not only dissatisfied workers but also the idle rich, gamblers and speculators, and women who marry for financial security. For all of these, "work is something hateful . . . money is desirable because it represents a way of escape from work. The only difference is that the rich have already made their escape and the poor have not."[21] The differing attitudes to work of the two groups affect what is manufactured and sold; both groups will need food, clothing and shelter; and materials for their work. They will also need things for their hours of leisure.

For the artist, and those who have good work, leisure is the interval that refreshes mind and body so that more of their own work might be done. Those who are satisfied with their work may have a taste for luxuries such as fine wines and gourmet food, as Sayers did; but they are not filling a void at the centre of their life, they are not trying to kill time or to create an identity for themselves. For the worker tied to work which is purely for a livelihood, leisure is an escape. If work is constitutive of personal identity, those who hate their work will probably be more open to the blandishments of the consumer society than those who find personal fulfilment in their work: "The commodities which it is easiest to advertise and sell are those which purport to 'take the work out' of everything . . . the commodities easiest to sell after the labour saving gadgets are the inventions for saving us from the intolerable leisure we have produced. . . . All our existence is an effort to escape from what we are doing."[22]

The reduction of leisure to "killing time" was, to Sayers, as dehumanising as the assembly line. People were not educated or encouraged to be independent, creative thinkers, but to be members of a herd easily swayed by the calls of the advertisers and propagandists. She wanted people to be

18. Sayers, *Unpopular Opinions*, 122.
19. Sayers, *Creed*, 47.
20. Ibid., 55.
21. Sayers, *Unpopular Opinions*, 123.
22. Sayers, "Vocation," 94.

active participants, mentally or physically, in their work and their leisure: "athleticism [is] preferable to passive amusement . . . games in which they had no share, or cinema where entertainment poured over their heads from a can."[23] Detective novels escape her condemnation because the reader is actively involved in the reading. Unlike Gill, who stated that if all things that are useful are made by machines, then "the blessing of leisure will turn into a curse of fretwork, and all sorts of amateur 'fancywork', fretwork and fretfulness,"[24] Sayers has time for amateurs, provided that they undertake to produce a good item which meets high standards for a thing of its kind.

Those who live to work instead of working to escape from work, find in their work intellectual and emotional interest and satisfaction. She gives lists of the workers she would classify in this group: artists, scholars, scientists, old fashioned craftsmen, skilled mechanics and engineers, doctors, priests, nurses, actors, teachers, seamen, farmers and farm-workers, airmen, explorers, and some wives and mothers. She distinguished between women who find childrearing a natural function and those who find it a vocation as she has described.[25]

Sayers had a framework for her concept of good work which was present in all her writings on work. She proposed that we should ask of any proposed work, either employment or leisure activity the following questions:

1. Is it useful?

2. Is it good?

3. Is it such that a man can properly dedicate his life to it?

4. Is it so arranged as to afford a right rhythm?

5. Are work and worker suited to each other?[26]

Sayers' made two major and related points: that the product should be worth making, addressed in questions one to three; and that the process of making should engage the creativity of the worker, questions three, four and five. Instead, the question has been "Does it pay?" Consequently, she noted, we have produced a wasteful society which failed to value the product, and "as a result it is a mockery to ask people to find vocation in

23. *Church Times*, "God and the Machine," 384.

24. Gill, *Work and Leisure*, 46.

25. Sayers, *Unpopular Opinions*, 123.

26. Sayers, "War and Post-War," 8.

work."[27] Individuals, the employer, the employed and the consumer must to be responsible agents, seeking good work, "work whose production and consumption can be a medium for praise to God."[28]

Sayers understood that work involved toil, jobs that are "hard, heavy, and disgusting, or monotonous and repetitive drudgery;"[29] "Work is notoriously a curse."[30] Workers could work with enthusiasm at such a job because they had a real conviction of the worth of the final product; even though they were doing the same repetitive, boring work, for example, the armament workers in the Tanks for Russia campaign.[31] She recognised that the worker must be suited to the task, and pointed out that some workers do not mind what others call drudgery. They should be allowed to have a job that suits their temperament, but it should still fit the natural rhythm of the human body, not the relentless pressure of the assembly line.

She used the artist for a guide to how work should be structured. She listed the privileges they enjoy in how they perform their work. First, their work provides opportunity for individual initiative; second, however laborious it may be in detail, it allows them to view with satisfaction the final results of their labour; and finally it is of a kind that fits in with the natural rhythm of the human mind and body and does not bind the worker to the monotonous, relentless, deadly pace of an inhuman machine.[32] These three characteristics should guide a reform of how work is done, that is how the assembly line is organised.

Certainly she would not reject a well-designed and well-made object because it was produced on an assembly line. She would reject the object that claimed superiority simply because it was hand-made without reference to its overall quality. Sayers did not advocate a return to a pre-industrial society as the Distributivists and the *Christendom* Group did. Such an attitude, she felt, was wrong because, "it takes no account of the real delight and satisfaction that the machines are capable of giving. It throws on the scrapheap the skill and creative enthusiasm of the designer, the engineer's

27. Ibid.
28. Sayers, "Work," 5.
29. Ibid., 7.
30. Sayers, *Unpopular Opinions*, 111.
31. Sayers, "Vocation," 97.
32. Sayers, *Unpopular Opinions*, 125.

pride in his craft . . . and all those products—and they are many—which are actually *better* made by machinery than by hand."[33]

The problem of the worker on an assembly line is that the task is designed so that the worker is reduced to a hand, an automaton. His or her creative powers are deliberately suppressed. Given Sayers' Trinitarian anthropology, this is clearly wrong, theologically and practically. It is possible to redesign their work so that it fits the three criteria she set out: to provide opportunity for individual initiative, to allow the worker to view with satisfaction the final result of their labour, and to fit the natural rhythm of human mind and body.

She believed that human ingenuity could learn to use the machines in a way that they would work in harmony with human nature instead of oppressing it. The structure of the workplace can be changed, Sayers claimed, if instead of viewing it as a question of economics we started with human nature and designed the manufacturing process around that. Sayers suggested that the real trouble with the machine age was that it had not yet advanced far enough; the machines might learn to feed themselves and only need "the skilled engineer, who might love it as an artist loved his picture."[34]

Sayers' criteria for good work are realistic, and, when implemented, they produced good economic results. Peter Drucker, in *The Practice of Management*, gave an example of a restructured manufacturing plant which follows Sayers' prescriptions, even though we have no evidence that he had read any of her work. In the factory producing aircraft-engine parts, the process was restructured so that one worker performed the eighty component operations to produce the complete part. "Much to everyone's surprise, this resulted in more, faster and better work than could possibly have been turned out either by highly skilled machinists or on the orthodox assembly line"[35] This would meet Sayers' standards allows the worker to perform a complete task at their own rhythm.

Drucker called designing work for humans integration. It begins with the analysis of the job according to the principles of Taylor's Scientific Management: analyse the job, improve overall performance by improving the performance of the individual motions or parts of the job, lay out the sequence of steps to be performed logically. The second step is the integration:

33. Ibid., 126.

34. *Church Times*, "Christianity and Leisure," 384.

35. Drucker, *Practice of Management*, 285.

"We know first that the job should constitute a distinct stage in the work process. The man—or the men—doing one job should always be able to see a result. It does not have to be a complete part. But it should always be a complete step. . . . Also the job should always depend for its speed and rhythm only on the performance of the man—or the men—performing it. . . . Finally . . . each job should embody some challenge, some element of skill or judgement."[36]

Richard Sennett documents the problems that occur when high-level application of technology to work removes all difficulty from production: the corporation can hire lower-skilled workers for lower pay, but the workers themselves are not involved in the process, and dissatisfied with their inability to intervene when the complex machinery malfunctions.[37] This encapsulates the major problem of modern global capitalism for most workers: their unique talents and skills are not needed. Work processes are not designed with the human workers in mind and fail to call upon their creativity.

It is possible for workplaces to be structured so that the work processes are designed with two of the qualifications that Sayers' specified: there is satisfaction in the final product and the rhythm of work fits the natural rhythm of the human mind and body, not the relentless unchanging pace of the machine. The allowance for individual initiative is more difficult. This requirement expresses the creativity she said was an essential part of human nature; and this is generally discouraged in most manufacturing processes where uniformity of final product is a high value. I was consulting at a plant manufacturing floor coverings which had recently installed a computer-controlled paint mixer to ensure that the contrast between production runs were minimal. However, the results were disappointing. The managers discovered the workers were still mixing the paints themselves; they were proud of their skill and wouldn't use the new equipment. If there is no option to exercise creativity, it is more difficult for a job to be satisfying.

Sayers conception of good work starts with work that makes a good product. Her standard is not unrealistic, Anthony in *The Ideology of Work* writes, 'Making things is also likely to be seen as purposeless activity if the things made are vulgar, trivial, or dangerous . . . If work is ever directed at the production of good and useful objects and at meeting important needs

36. Ibid., 289.
37. Sennett, *Corrosion of Character*, 72.

it may be restored in some sense to meaning."[38] Sayers does not give an adequate account of what a good product is. It may be that no such account is possible, especially if Sayers is right about creativity being a foundational part of human nature that humans must somehow express. Human beings have such varying needs, desires, and interests that what one person declares is shoddy trash, another person values. She depends on individual Christians to discern good products, and does not recommend any legislation or other restriction on what is made. At the same time she did not explicitly recognise that the demand that workers be creative in their work means that the economic system must have a high level of freedom with the consequence that the system will produce good and bad products.

She gave some general indications on what would qualify as a good product: it should be fit for the purpose, and should be honest. She condemned the jerry-built housing as "not only ugly but shoddy, not even well-designed for the most utilitarian purpose which a house can serve."[39] She called financial "trickeries" and "the manufacture of vulgar and useless trivialities" work which was a spiritual degradation.[40] She detailed what she considered worthless products: "china dogs, patent medicines, telephone-dolls, nail-varnishes, crooner-music, trash novels, and general rubbish and nonsense with which commerce has cluttered the world."[41] Her example of bad housing appeals to a clear standard, fitness for the purpose, and the example of financial trickeries to the standard of commercial honesty. The list of "tasteless and useful clutter" is open to the charge of snobbishness; the standard seems to be only the author's taste.

What is a good product is different for the writer as an artist as compared to the writer as a craftsman. As a writer, Sayers discussed integrity in work in terms of artistic integrity for the writer, which helps clarify her standards for a good product. She and C. S. Lewis had an exchange about the point of the artist's decision to accept work. He had accused her of using her artistic conscience to avoid doing things that didn't appeal to her, particularly apologetic work and public controversy. She claimed that a writer should not accept a commission to write about any subject the commissioner suggests, but only subjects which provide an opportunity for the writer to convey a truth: "If I have no truth asking to be communicated,

---

38. Anthony, *Ideology of Work*, 315–16.
39. Sayer, "Vocation," 99.
40. Sayers, *Creed*, 45.
41. Sayers, "Vocation," 99.

then neither the money, nor the hope of influencing people, or of giving pleasure, or fulfilling a demand, or anything else ought to weigh with me."[42] She had defined the artistic lie, saying it was "something in which the will does not assent to the undertaking."[43]

Yet Sayers herself had worked in advertising. She made her understanding of commercial honesty clear in a talk to Oxford undergraduates, "If you take money to write trash—even subversive trash—you must write what you are paid to write or give the money back."[44] Sayers' qualifications about the work an artist can accept with integrity did not exclude potboilers: she wrote *Murder Must Advertise* to boil the pot when *The Nine Tailors* took much longer to complete than she had expected. In a letter to Victor Gollancz about it she wrote, "The new book is nearly done. I hate it because it isn't the one I wanted to write, but I had to shove it in because I couldn't get the technical dope of the Nine Tailors in time." [45] Her comment in a letter to a fan shows her integrity in action, "The plot [of *Murder Must Advertise*] is rather hasty and conventional, because I wrote the book against time and rather against the grain; but the advertising part is sound enough."[46]

Part of integrity in work was craftsmanship, doing the work well technically. "[E]ven work done for pot-boiling should be done as well and as conscientiously as possible."[47] She wrote an ad for Horlicks using her character Lord Peter Wimsey in order to earn money to finance a tour of *The Zeal of Thy House*.[48] She compared factory work to an artist's pot-boiler.[49] She recognised that a great deal of work fell into this category. The task for the reformers is to arrange this work "so as to boil the pot as quickly as possible and in such a way that nobody's pot remains without a fire to boil it."[50]

Sayers insisted that "the worker's first duty is to *serve the work*,"[51] not keep one eye on the public. To do that is to encourage the artist to

42. Sayers, *Letters Vol. 3*, 256.

43. Ibid., 252.

44. Sayers, "Address," 4.

45. Sayers, *Letters Vol. 1*, 322–23.

46. Ibid., 330.

47. Sayers, "Plea for Vocation," 7.

48. Sayers, *Letters Vol. 2*, 98.

49. Sayers, "Vocation," 96–97.

50. Ibid.

51. Sayers, *Creed*, 62.

pander, and to produce false art: "We may say that the best Art should be recompensed at the highest rate, and no doubt it should; but if the artist lets his work be influenced by considerations of marketing, he will discover that what he is producing is not Art."[52]

If there is that happy congruence between the author's message and the audience, that is a West End hit; but to preserve his integrity the artist may not change what he wants to say into what he thinks the audience wants to hear. This is an acceptable standard for artists; but it is death to the small shopkeeper. Clearly different jobs will have standards of integrity; part of being a good merchant is knowing what products the public wants and what price they are willing to pay for them.

The idea of lay people finding their vocation in work was not unproblematic in Sayers' day or in ours. Demant pointed out that vocation was extended from the priesthood and religious life to marriage or "some occupation demanding special renunciations, such as the mission field, nursing and dangerous public services."[53] This, he points out, is a far cry from everyone's daily life; and we have "little reliable guidance in the historic tradition of the Church for deciding what vocation in work means"[54]

Sayers disagrees that only occupations with special renunciations are vocations. She wants everyone to see their work as a vocation; and chose work that is worthy of that name. She respected secular work. She claimed the church didn't respect the secular vocation and therefore the clerics excused bad workmanship: "Yet in her own buildings, in her own ecclesiastical art and music, in her hymns and prayers, in her sermons and in her little books of devotion, the Church will tolerate, or permit a pious intention to excuse, work so ugly, so pretentious, so tawdry and twaddling, so insincere and insipid, so bad as to shock and horrify any decent draftsman."[55]

The church often wanted work to edify, without understanding or respecting the artist's integrity:

> it is dangerous for anybody—even for the Church—to urge artists to produce works of art for the express purpose of "doing good to people." Let her by all means encourage artists to express their own Christian experience and communicate it to others. That is the true artist saying: "Look! recognise your experience as my

52. Ibid., 79.

53. Demant, *Theology of Society,* 176.

54. Ibid.

55. Sayers, *Why Work?* 16.

own." But "edifying art" may only too often be the pseudo-artist corruptly saying: "This is what you are supposed to believe and feel and do —and I propose to work you into a state of mind in which you will believe and feel and do as you are told." The pseudo-art does not really communicate power to us; it merely exerts power over us.[56]

Integrity in craftsmanship is more important than pious intentions: "Let us not disguise that an unsound play by a good dramatist will always be far more effective than an impeccably orthodox play by a bad dramatist."[57] The Church's failure to respect the secular vocation means that the "secular work of the world is turned to purely selfish and destructive ends, and that the greater part of the world's workers have become irreligious or at least, uninterested in religion."[58] The devaluation of the secular work was displayed, too, in the invitations Sayers received to do church work instead of her own work. In *Why Work?* she wrote, "when you find a man who is a Christian praising God by the excellence of his work—do not distract him and take him away from his proper vocation to address religious meetings and open church bazaars."[59]

Sayers' criteria for good work modelled on the artist—that it makes a product worth making, that it provides an opportunity for individual initiative and creativity; that however laborious it may be in detail, it allows the workers to view with satisfaction the final results of their labour; and finally that it is of a kind that fits in with the natural rhythm of human mind and body—do not specify the ownership of the means of production, the size or type of place where the work is done, or the social or economic framework within which the work is done. This seems to give insufficient weight to the effects of the institutional organisation of the economic sphere as a contributing factor to inhuman working conditions, or of the formation of the worker in the virtues of honesty and integrity. To fill out Sayers' account of good work, I turn to MacIntyre and his idea of a practice.

---

56. Sayers, *Unpopular Opinions*, 41.
57. Sayers, "Playwrights," 65.
58. Sayers, *Creed*, 58.
59. Sayers, *Why Work?* 18.

MacIntyre's Concept of a Practice

A practice is one of the three building blocks of MacIntyre's account of the virtues, an account which will, he says, lead us out of the moral wilderness. The practice is an essential constituent of MacIntyre's conception of virtue. A practice is "any coherent and complex form of socially established cooperative human activity through which goods internal to that form of activity are realized in the course of trying to achieve those standards of excellence which are appropriate to and partially definitive of, that form of activity, with the result that human powers to achieve excellence, and human conceptions of the ends and goods involved, are systematically extended."[60] The virtues are developed in practices, which form part of a human life which has the unity of a narrative, and the goal of discovering the good for a human.

Such lives are lived within traditions of moral reasoning. He wrote his account of practices in *After Virtue*. In *Dependent Rational Animals*, he uses the concept of a practice of the family to explore the process of humans becoming independent practical reasoners. He defended his concept of practices in articles responding to his critics; but I think it would be fair to say that although it is a building block of his theory, his attention, and his critics' attention, has been more focused on the idea of a tradition of rationality. In *Dependent Rational Animals*, his discussion of the virtues of acknowledged dependency, of children, of the sick and disabled, and of the old, are discussed within a naturalistic ethic.[61] This is an essential building block to the account of good work that will include the work of care.

He includes in his definition of practices fishing crews, farming families, string quartets, arts, sciences, games, politics in the Aristotelian sense, and the making and sustaining of family life.[62] This list is similar to the list of occupations that Sayers counts in the group of people who do have work fit for humans, artists, scholars, scientists, old fashioned craftsmen, skilled mechanics and engineers, doctors, priests, nurses, actors, teachers, seamen, farmers and farm-workers, airmen, explorers, and some wives and mothers. One key point of the definition for comparison with Sayers is the idea that the excellences, the ends and goods involved, are systematically

60. MacIntyre, *After Virtue*, 187.

61. MacIntyre, *Dependent*, x.

62. Ibid., 188. In "Practical Rationalities as Forms of Social Structure" he gives an expanded list of practices: "farming, war, poetry, drama, pursuit of gymnastic and athletic excellence, architecture, sculpture and painting, mathematics and theology," 4.

extended by those who participate in the practice: practices of their essence involve human creativity.[63]

In a practice, technical skills are needed, and rule-following is important for participants but they must develop their skills and reasoning powers to understand when they must go beyond the rules. This clarifies creativity as not as the freedom of liberalism, freedom from restraint, experienced as unrestricted activity or choices, but freedom in the natural law tradition, freedom for pursuit of the good.

Practices have internal and external goods, a distinction of critical importance for MacIntyre. This distinction clarifies Sayers' categorization of those who work for love of work, an internal good, and those who work to escape work, that is for money, an external good. External goods, money, power and fame, are contingently attached to the practice. An excellent portrait painter may find that his work, by virtue of its honesty in portraying character, an internal good of the practice of portrait painting, is unsalable, and his reputation non-existent, so he has none of the external goods of this practice. Furniture makers could be producing excellent furniture which cannot attract buyers at a price sufficient to afford the craftsmen a living wage; this could be the effect of a change in fashion in home decorating, an economic downturn, or the buyers' choice of furniture of lesser quality but a lower price. None of the factors are related to the quality of the furniture or under the control of the workers. The external good of the worker's wage is, as MacIntyre claimed, only contingently connected to the excellence of the work and its product. The external goods "are always some individual's property and possession" and MacIntyre claims that they are the kinds of things that, "the more someone has of them, the less there is for other people." [64] This is sometimes necessarily the case, as with power and fame, and sometimes the case by reason of contingent circumstance as with money. External goods are therefore characteristically objects of competition in which there must be losers as well as winners.

Internal goods of a practice are also the outcome of competition, but "their achievement is a good for the whole community who participate in the practice."[65] Sayers made a similar point when she discusses an artist's use of the word mine. When the artist sells a painting, we can say, in MacIntyre's terms, that the external sense of mine applies to the buyer; it is in-

63. MacIntyre, *After Virtue*, 193–94.

64. Ibid., 190.

65. Ibid., 190–91.

deed the buyer's picture. However, it has not ceased to be the artist's picture, the internal sense of the work mine. The internal goods of practices can be of two kinds. Using the example of portrait painting, MacIntyre identifies the first internal good as the excellence of the product, that is excellence in the painter's technique, and the excellence of the finished portrait. But a second internal good which a participant in this practice achieves or recognises is the good of a certain kind of life. It may not be the whole of life, but it means the person is now living part of their life "*as a painter*" [emphasis in original].[66]

This is one of, or possibly *the*, key feature of practices for MacIntyre's account of the virtuous life: participation in a practice involves the person in learning standards of excellence and rules, thus moving from an emotivist and subjective standard of judgement to an objective and shared standard. He writes "we have to accept as necessary components of any practice with internal goods and standards of excellence the virtues of justice, courage and honesty."[67] He writes that observers, those who appreciate good painting, (or a first rate experiment, or well-thrown passes) like active participants, can achieve the goods of the practices of painting (or physics, or American football) so long as they subordinate themselves within the practice in their relationships to other practitioners: their subjective judgement is not determinative of the good. Instead they must recognize what MacIntyre calls the necessary components of any practice, the virtues of honesty, courage and justice.[68]

Good work is work that is part of a practice, the school of virtue where participants pursue internal goods. MacIntyre rejects the fact/ value distinction which underlies modern economics, social science and therefore, much of the theory of management and organisation of modern workplaces. MacIntyre seems to restrict the idea of practice to small scale communities or worksites, and contrasts work in the household, a practice, and work in the public sphere of the factory and corporation:

> So long as productive work occurs within the structure of house-
> holds, it is easy and right to understand that work as part of the
> sustaining of the community of the household and of those wider
> forms of community. As, and to the extent that, work moves out-
> side the household and is put to the service of impersonal capital,

66. Ibid., 189–90.
67. Ibid., 190–91.
68. Ibid., 191.

> the realm of work tends to become separated from everything but the service of biological survival and the reproduction of the labor force, on the one hand, and that of institutionalized acquisitiveness, on the other.[69]

MacIntyre often refers to the family as a practice, sometimes as a tradition, sometimes as an institution and sometimes as a social context. Most times it is simply mentioned in the list of practices where the common good is pursued and practical enquiry occurs. The family is the primary and universal practice we experience among many practices in our lives.

The family is the practice that sustains and preserves the individual's life, where the plain person learns how to order ends rightly and as such is the basis for the training in practical reason that makes society possible.[70] Three primary virtues are developed out of the practice of family life: truthfulness; respect for, patience with, and care for the needs of others; and the faithful keeping of promises. These are the virtues that are necessary for any community to exist.

In *Dependent Rational Animals* MacIntyre details the process of becoming an independent practical reasoner, and the implications that has for the care of others. In so doing, he highlights the goods of the family as a practice, and the virtues that are required for the family to exist as a school of the virtues. The biological truth of the radical dependency of human infants is the starting point; a refreshing change from the moral philosophy that starts with the adult, autonomous individual. MacIntyre identifies childhood, old age and the experiences of disability and dependence at all stages of life, as neglected in moral philosophy. This is, I would suggest, one result of the gender roles that assigned women the care of all the dependents and men the work in the public sphere where questions of justice with other independent reasoners arise.

MacIntyre discusses the transition from infant to independent practical reasoner free from gender stereotyping. He identifies the infant experience of good—warmth, food, security, sleep—as pleasure in the satisfaction of bodily wants. To become an independent practical reasoner the infant and child must undergo a three-fold transition from the infant condition: first, an ability to step back and recognise different kinds of goods, evaluate different goods, recognise and deal with difficulties, and dangers; second, an ability to form cooperative relationships with others; and third, an ability

69. Ibid., 227.
70. MacIntyre, "Plain Persons," 140.

to be aware of the future, to hope.[71] The parents and teachers who cooperate in this process must have not only the virtues they are trying to inculcate, such as truthfulness, but also other virtues, such as a degree of care for the subject matter and for the student. The parental virtues called for by the infant are love and attention: they must be responsive, have an unconditional commitment to the child, and be non-retaliating. This is an unconditional commitment to this child even if it is ugly, sick or retarded; it is a decision to make the child's needs and not one's own needs paramount.[72]

MacIntyre's account of care relies on continuity between our animal nature and our rational capacity. He describes adult activity and belief as developing out of and continuous with modes of belief and activity that we share with other species of intelligent animals.[73] Janet Martin Soskice in her article "Love and Attention" would agree, and uses the example of a mother's response of lactation to her baby's cry, or what she thinks is her baby's cry, as "*both involuntary and rational*, dependent as it is on the mother's beliefs."[74] She writes "To be fully human and to be fully moral is to respond to that which demands our response—the other, attended to with love."[75] Her account of the love and attention a child demands, like MacIntyre's account of care, is not gender-specific unless there is an essential biological component, such as lactation. It matches MacIntyre's too, and joins it in opposition to a morality of calculation of benefits, even when presented with the radically dependent, the sick, the old, the disabled. The dichotomy of relationships which are either governed by bargaining for mutual advantage, or relationships which are governed by affection, is not enough. The existence of the human need demands our response; the need is the determinative criteria to judge the morality of our response. MacIntyre sums this up in his example of a man walking into his local butcher shop, seeing the butcher suffering a heart attack and saying, "Ah, not in a position to sell me my meat today, I see."[76]

The rational consumer, concerned only with satisfying his or her wants, would take the steak, leave the price, and leave. The virtuous shopper responds to the butcher's need, calling an ambulance. This action does

71. MacIntyre, *Dependent*, 72–74.

72. Ibid., 91.

73. Ibid., 41.

74. Soskice, "Love and Attention," 69.

75. Ibid., 67.

76. MacIntyre, *Dependent*, 117.

not easily fit into the virtues of justice, temperance, prudence, or courage, as we commonly define them; it is an example of what MacIntyre calls the virtues of acknowledged dependence. These are the virtues of giving and receiving which require us in our giving to be just, generous, beneficent, sensitive to others' suffering, and taking action to relieve it. They also encompass the virtues of receiving: exhibiting gratitude without it becoming a burden, extending courtesy towards the graceless giver and forbearance towards the inadequate giver, and making a truthful acknowledgment of dependence, thus giving up our illusions of self-sufficiency.[77] This account of these virtues, based on a fuller description of human life and human moral agents than the autonomous adult individual of much Enlightenment moral philosophy, gives us an account of the ethics of care that is gender neutral.

MacIntyre's account of the family as a practice completes and clarifies Sayers' account of good work. MacIntyre describes work within the household, whatever that work may be, as the practice of sustaining the household community. Although he does not make it explicit, considering the pre-industrial economy, the work of the household would seem to be farming or a craft, and in any case at least some food production. Sayers would agree that the household producing its own food, drink, clothing and medicines was a place of creative work as well as of toil and drudgery. Her criticism of assigning women only to the household in the industrial economy was threefold: first, that industrialisation had strengthened gender stereotypes which harmed women and men. Sayers wanted both men and women to have good work in their lives, "Every woman is a human being—one cannot repeat that too often—and a human being must have occupation, if he or she is not to become a nuisance to the world."[78] Jobs should be allotted to those who have the desire, skills and talents to fulfil them, without first asking about gender. Second, she was particularly critical of the ideal of the "lady of the house" as the idle woman, who doesn't soil her hands with work. Third, the rewarding jobs, baking, brewing, and textile crafts, for example, were taken out of the household and into the factory which left women the toil of cleaning and the task of consuming.[79]

Sayers' recognised that caring for children was creative work, and fulfilling work for many women, but a burden for others who lacked the

77. Ibid., 126–27.
78. Sayers, *Unpopular Opinions*, 110.
79. Ibid., 109–10.

patience, tolerance of disorder and attention to detail to fully engage with babies and small children. What she asks is that the job come first: "Once lay down the rule that the job comes first and you throw that job open to every individual, man or woman, fat or thin, tall or short, ugly or beautiful, who is able to do that job better than the rest of the world."[80]

Women have a special role in pregnancy and lactation; but most of the work of care for children, the sick and the elderly does not have that kind of biological tie to a single sex. Much care is first of all presence, attentiveness to the person. Recognising the biological necessities and dismantling the socially constructed roles of wallet and womb free men and women for a more human life.

Sayers' writings on work depend on the adult Christian's virtue, but she gives no account of how that virtue develops. MacIntyre does give such an account, an account which recognises the reality of gender without perpetuating the assignment of women to the home simply because they are women while at the same time excusing men from the virtues of acknowledged dependence. MacIntyre's household requires all members, male and female to participate in the practice of creating the human community of family.

A good human life for human beings, according to Sayers, consists of "interesting occupation, reasonable freedom for their pleasures, and a sufficient emotional outlet. What form the occupation, the pleasures and the emotion may take, depends entirely upon the individual"[81] Her definition of "interesting occupation," that is good work, is work that makes a product worth making, produced in a way that provides an opportunity for individual initiative and creativity; that however laborious it may be in detail, allows the workers to view with satisfaction the final results of their labour; and that fits in with the natural rhythm of human mind and body. Her focus is on the individual, calling each person to be responsible for their own actions and not to be a passive observer manipulated by economic, political or religious forces. Her starting anthropology is that each person bears the image of the Trinitarian God in their ability to create. Her analogy sees humanity as essentially social rather than isolated, autonomous individuals.

Macintyre's work in his *After Virtue* project highlights the bankruptcy of a moral philosophy which is cut off from history and community. He describes the good human life as a life lived in pursuit of the good for humans

80. Ibid., 110.
81. Ibid., 114.

through participation in practices, human communities which form individuals in the virtues of justice, courage, honesty and the recognition of responsibility to those who are dependent. The latter point is inherent in the idea of a household as a practice which he developed in *Dependent Rational Animals*. Good work is work within a practice whereby the individual learns the virtues by seeking the internal goods of the practice, and by exercising creativity, expands the bounds of the practice.

MacIntyre expands Sayers' account of leisure. She identified playing a sport as good leisure, being an observer of the game as a passive, and therefore a less worthwhile activity. MacIntyre recognises playing a sport as participating in a practice, but he extends this to certain observers. He distinguishes two kinds of observer. The first might be called the consumer, there to seek nothing beyond his personal pleasure, that is, his subjective judgement of the good. The other, the fan, is participating in the practice of the sport, recognizing a human community that has shared standards of judgment of good rather than a collection of individual emotivist judgements of good. This standard can be applied to other activities such as going to the movies; it can be a passive activity of killing time, or it can be a practice for those who are willing to recognise a standard of good in writing, in cinematography, in acting, that is not just their personal preference.

MacIntyre describes most of the work done by people in the modern world as outside the realm of practices for two reasons. First, he places the economic realm outside the realm of practices, since it is governed in liberal capitalism by the idea of a person as an autonomous individual, not a member of a community. Second, he claims that work in the modern economy cannot be understood as having internal goods, only external goods: "There is no relationship of desert or merit connecting work and its products on the one hand and endeavour and skill on the other"[82]

Practices are sustained by institutions, the "social bearers of the practices"[83] which are at the same time in conflict with the practices. The chess club, the university, the hospital, these are the institutions concerned with the external goods of chess, philosophy and medicine. The institution and the practice "characteristically form a single causal order in which the ideals and the creativity of the practice are always vulnerable to the

---

82. MacIntyre, "Rights, Practices," 245.
83. MacIntyre, *After Virtue*, 195.

acquisitiveness of the institution."[84] The virtues of justice, courage and honesty enable practices to resist the corrupting power of institutions.

Institutions and Managers

The institutions of modern capitalism, the corporation and the bureaucratic state are concerned with external goods of power, status, and money. MacIntyre condemns modern politics and economics, because they are conceived as value-free or value-neutral spheres within which autonomous individuals exercise their personal preferences. As such they cannot be practices, cannot educate participants in the virtues. In *After Virtue*, the manager was a representative character of modernity and shown as claiming two things: neutrality and effectiveness. MacIntyre would maintain these are moral fictions to hide the raw exercise of power. If managers respond that his characterisation of them is a straw man, and that they do not make any claims to neutrality or to knowing or relying on law-like generalisations of social science but instead make the modest claim of competence and expertise in a particular field, he replies, "it is not claims of this kind which achieve power . . . For claims of this modest kind could never legitimate the possession or the uses of power either within or by bureaucratic corporations in anything like the way or on anything like the scale on which that power is wielded."[85]

To MacIntyre their modest claims are not a rebuttal of his argument, but an excuse to participate in the charade of corporate life.[86] MacIntyre rejects the anthropology of the autonomous individual and modern liberal capitalism's conception of the common good as constructed out of the sum of the goods of individuals. The goods which are being summed are those MacIntyre characterises as only external goods. Since external goods are the property of individuals, rather than goods held in common, competitiveness is the dominant feature of this society. The competitiveness corrupts the communal ties, and ensures that such a society cannot be virtuous. MacIntyre would reject the idea that workers in the modern corporations and the bureaucracies of the state could be participating in practices; and that being the case, they are not doing good work.

84. Ibid., 194.
85. Ibid., 108.
86. Ibid.

MacIntyre and Sayers would agree that the modern mass production economy is based on avarice, covetousness, and envy. Sayers, living through the world depression, could not conceive of the machines running to provide full employment without either wasteful consumption or war. Whoever owned the machines, the capitalist or the state, faced the same dilemma.[87] Consumption had to be artificially stimulated, and that meant, according to Sayers, that society was "founded on trash and waste."[88] Sayers saw the entire system resting on individuals acting as members of the unthinking herd, rather than as responsible producers and consumers: "We could—you and I—bring the whole fantastic economy of profitable waste down to the ground overnight, without legislation and without revolution, merely by refusing to cooperate with it."[89]

Her criticism of large bureaucratic organisations, whether businesses or government agencies, was that they institutionalised the uncreative, problem/solution mentality which will "falsify our apprehension of life as disastrously as they falsify our apprehension of art."[90] This may seem like a minor criticism, compared to MacIntyre's indictment of liberal capitalism, but it resonates with his understanding that practices are embodied in institutions. If the corporation embodies the social contract theory, the bureaucratic institutions whether of the state, charity sector, or a large business embody the problem/solution mentality within norms of justice of the society.[91] It is a legitimate criticism to ask if innovation and creativity can function within large organisations which define the good as following procedure.

Sayers criticized the basis for industrial society, "production is for the sake of the consumer," as a half-truth resulting from thinking of work in terms of serving society.[92] This way of looking at things meant that we did not see that we are all consumers and therefore should all be producers according to our abilities, and that it "imposes no responsibility on each of us as [a] consumer to see that he consumes and desires worthy things. Production is for producer and consumer alike, so that both may

---

87. Sayers, *Creed*, 52.
88. Ibid., 47.
89. Ibid., 52.
90. Sayers, *Mind of the Maker*, 194.
91. Sayers, *Letters Vol. 2*, 147, and "Wimsey Papers," 672.
92. Sayers, "Work," 5.

live well according to their nature."[93] When consumers do not accept their responsibility to choose good products, "we manufacture employment by manufacturing a demand for evil things" such as "the shoddy, the vulgar, the pornographic, the trivial."[94]

MacIntyre criticises the underlying philosophy of the institutions which embody social contract theory which see autonomous individuals as trying to maximize their preference-satisfaction; the common good is no more than fair rules for participants to bargain over the satisfaction of their preferences. In such a system each person is left "free both to calculate what is in my own best interest and to choose what my affective ties to others shall be."[95] This view is defective in that all relationships are categorized as either relationships undertaken for mutual advantage (the market paradigm) or relationships of affection which I choose to acknowledge. This dichotomy omits the kind of relationships of giving and receiving that actually make human life possible. Affective relationships are more than contractual relationships or accidents of congruence of emotions; these relationships of choice, MacIntyre claims, are "embedded in and sustained by relationships governed by norms of uncalculated and unpredicted giving and receiving."[96]

While both Sayers and MacIntyre see the problems with a public morality of procedural rules within which individuals seek their personal preferences, and the institutions this produces, Sayers would make individuals responsible for recognising how defective this conception is rather than making a general criticism of the institutions of capitalism. Sayers seems to rely on individuals' being educated in the virtues by the family and the church without making that process explicit. I suggest that this is partly a result of the time when she was writing, and her agenda in freeing women from the gender role which restricted them to the home.

MacIntyre gives an account of the process which could produce an individual with the ability to judge just how defective this conception is, and how necessary the virtues of dependence are. He gives an account of how the family, groups in the society, and practices form a person in the virtues. He claims that such groups and the institutions which support practices must be small-scale to be effective. MacIntyre sees the good work as work

---

93. Ibid.
94. Ibid.
95. MacIntyre, *Dependent*, 114.
96. Ibid., 119.

within practices, which includes creativity; Sayers sees good work as work that uses human creativity to make a worthwhile product wherever that work takes place.

Sayers' idea of the essential creative dimension of good work is not dependent upon the setting, for her understanding depends on an initial theological commitment to a Triune Creator God who has made humans in his likeness in a world where God Himself took flesh. This makes all human work potentially good whatever the institutional setting. Judging work as good will depend on the quality of the work, the skill of the workman and the quality of the product; the motivation for the work; the reward sought for the work and the effect of the work on the worker and the society. Sayers criticizes bureaucracy wherever it is found, in a corporation, in a charity, in a government. Sayers' sees the lay Christian's vocation as the secular work he or she is called upon to perform.

If MacIntyre is correct, first, that good work is work within a practice and second, that practices cannot be sustained within the modern institutions of the corporation, or the modern liberal democratic state, then only smallholding farmers, craftsmen, artists and scientists are performing good work. However, since he allows institutions such as the university and the hospital as institutions which support practices, his ideas about institutions need further examination. MacIntyre's examples of institutions, the university, the hospital and the chess club, are non-profit organisations. However, the state bureaucracy shares with these organisations an existence outside the economic competition for profit, and in MacIntyre's view does not sustain politics as a practice.

MacIntyre also would not regard a corporation as an institution which can sustain practices, because it is concerned with external goods only. Sayers would suggest that responsible individuals could act virtuously within these institutions. It is my contention that taking Sayers' idea of individual responsibility seriously means that corporations and bureaucracies can be institutions which may house but not sustain practices.

The human beings who are formed in the virtues in their household, schools, religious organisations and neighbourhood groups can bring to institutions the practice of sustaining a human community. If they succeed, they do so despite institutional obstacles. The basic virtues, honesty and justice, are necessary for any human community, and within large institutions small groups may form which then act as the community. This may be a department in a large comprehensive school which is united about the teaching goals and goods; the project team or a small branch office of a large corporation, or the committees of the trade union in a large industrial plant. What I am suggesting is that people in an impersonal, de-humanising environment will work to create structures which allow them to experience community, although many times the rules of the organisation will render their efforts void.

An example which illuminates the differences of cultures between organisations is found in the work of Roger Bolton and Dorothy Grover Bolton. They observed that their work, training in communication skills, resulted in good productivity gains in some organisations, and few gains in others. Since the same techniques and materials were used in every organisation, they undertook further investigation to discover what made the difference in the changes to productivity in different organisations. They concluded that three basic virtues are required for constructive relationships within organisations which translated better communication into productivity gains: honesty, respect, and fairness.[97] This confirms Sayers' insight that the individual's action is significant, which Drucker emphasised when he discussed the character of the manager: "A man might himself know too little, perform poorly, lack judgement and ability, and yet not do damage as a manager. But if he lack in character and integrity – no matter how knowledgeable, how brilliant, how successful—he destroys. He destroys people, the most valuable resource of the enterprise. He destroys spirit. And he destroys performance."[98]

MacIntyre and Sayers complement each other. Both recognise the essential element of creativity in good work; both see work as an essential part of human flourishing, and not just a punishment for sin. Sayers writes about the obligations of responsible adult individuals without any account of their formation in the virtues. MacIntyre's account of the virtues of acknowledged dependency opens a new framework for connecting the family and the workplace, and the moral theology of the virtues and vices and the social ethics of natural law. MacIntyre's and Sayers' critique of bureaucracy hints at a way to ensure that the small scale communities which sustain practices and form virtuous individuals can be protected, to the benefit of the individuals, of institutions, and of the larger society.

97. Bolton, *People Skills*, 110–12.
98. Drucker, *Practice*, 193.

Conclusion: Good Work,
Christian Vocation and Social Institutions

This chapter opened with three problems for any theology of work in the contemporary world: the gender roles of the separate spheres, secular work and Christian vocation, and inhuman work. The Trinitarian understanding of the person that Sayers is proposing immediately shows the person as relational, re-connects the dimension of creativity in the person and in social ethics with the systematic theology of the Trinity. A proper understanding of the Trinity shows us a radical equality between persons. This is the first move toward ending the division of work into "separate spheres" with women assigned to childbearing and childrearing. Work is about human beings. From this starting point, we can examine the family and the work of care in a clearer way.

MacIntyre's work on the family and the virtues of acknowledged dependency forms a basis to speak of the work of care, particularly within the family, in a way which does not rely on gender stereotypes. Human beings in the practice of the family learn to sustain the human community and acquire the virtues of acknowledged dependency. These are the virtues of care which responds to human need *qua* need, and receives care from others with gratitude. His account does not assign these virtues solely to women while men are in the public sphere pursuing justice; he requires all human beings to acknowledge their dependence on others and to grow in these virtues. Motherhood is valued, and fatherhood is recovered as a human relationship, rather than simply a financial obligation.

The relation of secular work to Christian vocation is one of Sayers' core concerns. In her speeches and writings she asks the Church to respect the secular vocation, first by not seeing lay peoples' lives as divided between service to mammon and service to God but seeing that "every maker or worker is called to serve God in his profession or trade—not outside it."[99] For the laity, their secular work is their divine vocation. This involves respecting the autonomy of the secular sphere: "the living and eternal truth is expressed in work only so far as that work is true in itself, to itself, to the standards of its own technique." The Church's job, in Sayers' view, was to "see to it that the workers are Christian people," by this she means more than an individual supplied with a checklist of sins to avoid. [100]

99. Sayers, *Creed,* 59.
100. Ibid.

Sayers and MacIntyre offer a human vision of work developed from their experiences as a writer and a philosopher. Their conception gives primacy to creativity, and judges work to be fit for humans as it allows those humans to develop their creative powers in a community. From this starting point Sayers develops a way of designing work for humans. She gave three general standards for job design: work should provide an opportunity for individual initiative and creativity, that it should allow the worker to view a satisfactory result of their work, and it should fit the rhythm of the human body. Her discussions of job design were prescient of many changes made to the workplace. Sayers criticised the consumer society for producing a superabundance of superfluities and trash. To counteract this, Sayers relies on the individual acting responsibly within a consumerist society, choosing good work and choosing to spend wisely. Her standard for determining if a product is good requires a person formed in the virtues. She gave not account of that formation as MacIntyre did.

Sayers offered a general criticism of bureaucracy as embodying a problem/solution mentality which hinders human creativity. MacIntyre criticised the institutions of liberal capitalism, the corporation and the political institutions as being based on a false understanding of the person and consequently of the common good. Sayers' Trinitarian anthropology and her understanding of work fit for such a worker refine MacIntyre's idea of the practice in such a way that it becomes relevant to workers in all types of economic organisations, state bureaucracies, corporations or small entrepreneurial enterprises. The key is reading "goods internal to the practice" in the terms Sayers describes when she speaks of the worker serving the work.

Businesses as institutions in modern capitalism work against creating a community of virtue. Sayers' idea of the individual's responsibility and therefore of the possibility for the individual to resist the corrupting power of institutions means that individuals within organisations, whether state bureaucracies or business enterprises can live as a virtuous persons and create and sustain human community, often in the face of institutional obstacles. The only way this can come about is if the people who make up the business are formed in the virtues and see their work as part of redeeming the world. Sayers and MacIntyre read together show how this can come to be.

APPENDIX I

The Joint Letter on the Five Peace Points

21 December 1940 *The Times*

SIR,

The present evils in the world are due to the failure of nations and peoples to carry out the laws of God. No permanent peace is possible in Europe unless the principles of the Christian Religion are made the foundation of national policy and of all social life. This involves regarding all nations as members of one family under the Fatherhood of God.

We accept the five points of Pope Pius XII as carrying out this principle (see The Pope's Five Peace Points, pp. 13–16):

1. The assurance to all nations of their right to life and independence. The will of one nation to live must never mean the sentence of death passed upon another. When this equality of rights has been destroyed, attacked, or threatened, order demands that reparation shall be made, and the measure and extent of that reparation is determined, not by the sword nor by the arbitrary decision of self-interest, but by the rules of justice and reciprocal equity.

2. This requires that the nations be delivered from the slavery imposed upon them by the race for armaments and from the danger that material force, instead of serving to protect the right, may become an overbearing and tyrannical master. The order thus established requires a

mutually agreed organic progressive disarmament, spiritual as well as material, and security for the effective implementing of such an agreement.

3. Some juridical institution which shall guarantee the loyal and faithful fulfilment of conditions agreed upon and which shall in case of recognised need revise and correct them.

4. The real needs and just demands of nations and populations and racial minorities to be adjusted as occasion may require, even where no strictly legal right can be established, and a foundation of mutual confidence to be thus laid, whereby many incentives to violent action will be removed.

5. The development among peoples and their rulers of that sense of deep and keen responsibility which weighs human statutes according to the sacred and inviolable standards of the laws of God. They must hunger and thirst after justice and be guided by that universal love which is the compendium and most general expression of the Christian ideal.

With these basic principles for the ordering of international life we would associate five standards by which economic situations and proposals may be tested (see *The Churches Survey Their Task*, pp. 116, 117):

6. Extreme inequality in wealth and possessions should be abolished.

7. Every child, regardless of race or class, should have equal opportunities for education, suitable for the development of his peculiar capacities.

8. The family as a social unit must be safeguarded.

9. The sense of the Divine vocation must be restored to man's daily work.

10. The resources of the earth should be used as God's gifts to the whole human race and used with due consideration for the needs of the present and future generations.

We are confident that the principles which we have enumerated would be accepted by rulers and statesmen throughout the British Commonwealth of Nations and would be regarded as the true basis on which a lasting peace could be established.

Cosmo Cantuar, Archbishop of Canterbury
A. Cardinal Hinsley, Archbishop of Westminster
Walter H. Armstrong, Moderator Free Church Federal Council
William Ebor, Archbishop of York.

APPENDIX II

Christ the Worker a Dogmatic Approach

The suggestion [of dedicating a church or a church feast day to Christ Carpenter] was made in the course of a paper read at Brighton on the subject of Point 9 of the Churches' Manifesto: 'That the sense of a Divine vocation must be restored to man's daily work.' My approach to the question was dogmatic, and involved the following positions:

1. That God is the maker of the universe and God the Son the Divine Energy (or "Heavenly Worker") *per quem omnia facta sunt.*

2. That Man is made in the image of his Creator, and that a creative spirit in his work is part of his Divine likeness.

3. That the curse laid upon Adam was not work (Gen. ii.15) but work for a livelihood (Gen. iii. 19) so that he might no longer work, as God works, solely for the joy in creation and love of the thing made.

   (Here we part company from the Communist, for whom the economic factor gives to work its prime sanction, value and dignity.)

4. That when Man's labour and the earth's resources are exploited to economic ends, joy in creation is made impossible. Man's proper nature is thwarted and corrupted, and sacrilege is committed against God's whole creation.

5. As corollary: that the right understanding of a Divine vocation in work demands (a) a sacramental reverence for the material body of God's universe, and (b) a stipulation that the work men are called on to do shall be both worth doing and well done.

6. That Jesus Christ the Carpenter, as He is the Incarnation, is also for us the symbol, of the Eternal Worker, immanent in the world which He transcends.

7. Accordingly, that a devotion to "Christ Carpenter" (*Christus Opifex*) should operate to impress on Christian minds certain dogmas, which run the risk of being neglected, concerning (a) the nature of God, (b) the true nature of Man, (c) the right relation between Man and the material universe.

Nothing in all this, of course, in any way opposes the "work" of the Carpenter's Shop to the "work" of the Ministry. The habit of drawing a distinction between manual and mental labour is part or the unsacramental attitude to life which makes an unreal division between "practical" and "spiritual" religion, and (in secular affairs) between "learned" and "technical" education. The Incarnate Logos and the working Carpenter are not two but one and the same Heavenly Worker, indivisible in all His words and works. . . .

Bibliography

Augustine. *De Trinitate*. Online: http://www.newadvent.org/fathers/1301.htm.

Anthony, P. D. *The Ideology of Work*. London: Tavistock, 1977.

Bell, George. Papers relating to the Sword of the Spirit. Lambeth Palace Archive Vol. 71.

———. Sayers Correspondence. Lambeth Palace Archive Vol. 208 ff. 244–302.

Bolton, Roger, and Dorothy G. *People Styles at Work. Making Bad Relationships Good and Good Relationships Better*. New York: Amacom, 1996.

Borne, Etienne, and François Henry. *A Philosophy of Work*. Translated by F. Jackson. London: Sheed & Ward, 1938.

Brabazon, James. *Dorothy L. Sayers: A Biography*. London: Victor Gollancz, 1981.

Bray, Suzanne. "Introduction." In *Les Origines du Roman Policier: A Wartime Talk to the French*, by D. L. Sayers. Translated by Suzanne Bray. Hurstpierpoint: The Dorothy L. Sayers Society, 2003.

Brown, David. *The Divine Trinity*. London: Duckworth, 1985.

———. "The Trinity in Art." In *The Trinity: An Interdisciplinary Symposium on the Trinity*, edited by Stephen T. Douglas et al., 329–56. Oxford: Oxford University Press, 1999.

British Council of Churches. *The Forgotten Trinity*. Edited by Alasdair Heron. London: BCC/CCBI, 1991.

Caine, Barbara. *English Feminism 1780–1980*. Oxford: Oxford University Press, 1997.

Catholic Herald. "Christian Order for Britain." May 16, 1941.

The Church Times. "The Call for a Christian New Order." May 16, 1941, 282.

———. "God and the Machine." July 10, 1942, 384.

———. "Imaginative Theology: Miss Sayers's Latest Thriller." September 19, 1941, 537.

———. "Tirade Against Trash." February 13, 1942, 101.

Conlan, T. J., SJ. Review of *The Mind of the Maker* by Dorothy L. Sayers. *The Dublin Review* (1943): 87–90.

Craig, Robert. *Social Concern in the Thought of William Temple*. London: Victor Gollancz, 1963.

Crockford's Clerical Directory. Supplement to 1941. Oxford: Oxford University Press., 1942.

Davis, Stephen T., et al. *The Trinity: An Interdisciplinary Symposium on the Trinity*. Oxford: Oxford University Press, 1999.

Demant, V. A. *The Religious Prospect*. London: Frederich Muller, 1939.

———. *Theology of Society: More Essays in Christian Polity*. London: Faber & Faber, 1947.

Drucker, Peter. *The End of Economic Man: A Study of the New Totalitarianism*. London: William Heinemann, 1939.

———. *The Practice of Management*. Oxford: Elsevier Butterworth-Heinemann, 2005.

Dulles, Avery, SJ. *The Craft of Theology: From Symbol to System. Towards a Postcultural Theology*. New York: Crossroads, 1992.

Edwards, Ruth Dudley. *Matricide at St Martha's*. London: HarperCollins, 1994.

Gill, Eric. *Work and Leisure*. London: Faber & Faber, 1935.

Gunton, Colin E. *The One, the Three and the Many: God, Creation and the Culture of Modernity The Bampton Lectures 1992*. Cambridge: Cambridge University Press, 1993.

———, editor. *God and Freedom: Essays in Historical and Systematic Theology*. Edinburgh: T. & T. Clark, 1995.

Haack, Susan. 'After My Own Heart: Dorothy L. Sayers's Feminism." *New Criterion* 19 (2001). Online: http://ezproxy.umuc.edu/login?url=http://search.epnet.com/login. aspx?direct=true&db=aph&an=4807273.

Hastings, Adrian. *A History of English Christianity 1920–1990*. London: SCM, 1991.

Heilbrun, Carolyn. *Writing a Woman's Life*. London: Woman's, 1988.

Hill, William J. *The Three-personed God: The Trinity as a Mystery of Salvation*. Washington, DC: Catholic University of America Press, 1982.

Hodgson, Leonard. *The Doctrine of the Trinity Croall Lectures 1942–43*. London: Nisbet, 1943.

Horne, Brian. "Art: A Trinitarian Imperative." In *Trinitarian Theology Today Essays on Divine Being and Act*, edited by Christoph Schwöbel, 80–91. Edinburgh: T. & T. Clark, 1995.

Kenney, Catherine. *The Remarkable Case of Dorothy L. Sayers*. Kent, OH: The Kent State University Press, 1990.

LaCugna, Catherine M. *God for Us: The Trinity and Christian Life*. New York: HarperSanFrancisco, 1991.

Lang, Cosmo, A. Hinsley, W. Armstrong, and W. Temple. "Joint Letter." *The Times*, December 21, 1940.

Lewis, C. S. Review of *The Mind of the Maker* by Dorothy L. Sayers. *Theology* 43 (1941): 248–49.

Lindbeck, George A. *The Nature of Doctrine Religion and Theology in a Postliberal Age*. Philadelphia: Westminster, 1984.

Lloyd, Roger. *The Church of England 1900–1965*. London: SCM, 1966.

Loades, Ann. *Feminist Theology Voices from the Past*. Cambridge, UK: Polity, 2001.

———. *Spiritual Writings Dorothy l. Sayers*. London: SPCK, 1993.

MacIntyre, Alasdair. *After Virtue*. 2nd ed. Notre Dame, IL: University of Notre Dame Press, 1984.

———. *Dependent Rational Animals: Why Human Beings Need the Virtues*. Chicago: Open Court, 1999.

———. "Plain Persons and Moral Philosophy: Rules, Virtues and Goods." In *The MacIntyre Reader*, edited by K. Knight, 136–52. Cambridge, UK: Polity, 1998.

———. "Politics, Philosophy and the Common Good." In *The MacIntyre Reader*, edited by K. Knight, 235–52. Cambridge, UK: Polity, 1998.

———. "Rights, Practices and Marxism: Reply to Six Critics." *Analyse und Kritik 7*, (1985) 234–48.

Martin, Francis. *The Feminist Question: Feminist Theology in the Light of Christian Tradition.* Edinburgh: T. & T. Clark, 1994.

Mascall, Eric L. *The Triune God an Ecumenical Study.* Worthing: Churchman, 1986.

Mid-Sussex Times. "Miss Dorothy Sayers 'Preaches a Sermon.'" September 23, 1941.

Milton, John. *Paradise Lost.* Online: http://www.gutenberg.org/ebooks/20.

Moloney, Thomas. *Westminster, Whitehall and the Vatican: the Role of Cardinal Hinsley 1935–43.* Tunbridge Wells: Burns & Oates, 1985.

Murphy, Mark C., editor. *Alasdair MacIntyre.* Cambridge: Cambridge University Press, 2003.

Oldham, J. H., editor. *The Christian Newsletter.* No 1, October. 1939.

———. *The Christian Newsletter.* No. 83, May 28, 1941.

———. *The Christian Newsletter.* No. 194, November 3, 1943.

Oliver, John. *The Church and Social Order: Social Thought in the Church of England 1918–1939.* London: A. R. Mowbray, 1968.

O'Neill, Mary Aquin. "The Mystery of Being Human Together." In *Freeing Theology: The Essentials of Theology in Feminist Perspective,* edited by Catherine Mowry LaCugna, 139–60. San Francisco: HarperSanFrancisco, 1993.

Pope Pius XII. *Quadragesimo Anno.* Encyclical Letter. 15 May 1931. http://www.vatican.va/holy_father/pius_xi/encyclicals/documents/hf_p-xi_enc_19310515_quadragesimo-anno_en.html.

Preston, Ronald. "A Century of Anglican Social Thought." *The Modern Churchman* (March 1943) 337–47.

———. "The Malvern Conference." *The Modern Churchman* (April 1942) 15–22.

R., G. R. Review of *The Mind of the Maker* by Dorothy Sayers. *The Downside Review,* No. 180 LXIX (October 1941) 441–47.

Rahner, Karl. *The Trinity.* London: Burns & Oates, 1970.

Ramsey, Arthur Michael. *From Gore to Temple The Development of Anglican Theology between* Lux Mundi *and the Second World War 1889-1939. The Hale Memorial Lectures of Seabury-Western Theological Seminary, 1959.* London: Longmans, 1960.

Ratzinger, Joseph. "Concerning the Notion of Person in Theology." *Communio* (Fall 1990) 439–545.

Raven, Charles. "COPEC Then and Now." *Crucible* (January 1963) 10–14.

Reckitt, Maurice. *Christendom* Reviews. *Christendom,* June, 1940, 133.

Reynolds, Barbara. *Dorothy L Sayers Her Life and Soul.* London: Hodder & Stoughton, 1993.

Richardson, Cyril Charles. *The Doctrine of the Trinity.* New York: Abingdon, 1958.

Sayers, Dorothy Leigh. "Address to Undergraduates." MS 3. n. d. The Marion E. Wade Center, Wheaton College, Wheaton, IL.

———. "Aristotle on Detective Fiction." *English* 1.1 (1936) 23–35.

———. *Begin Here.* London: Victor Gollancz, 1939.

———. *Busman's Honeymoon.* With M. Byrne. In *Love All: Together with Busman's Honeymoon.* Edited by Alzina Dale. Kent State, OH: Kent State University Press. 1984.

———. *Busman's Honeymoon.* London: Victor Gollancz. 1937.

———. *Catholic Tales and Christian Songs.* Oxford: McBride. 1918.

———. "Cat O'Mary." In *Dorothy L. Sayers Child and Woman of Her Time,* edited by Barbara Reynolds, 25–159. Hurstpierpoint, West Sussex: The Dorothy L. Sayers Society, 2002.

———. *The Christ of the Creeds, and Other Broadcast Messages to the British People during World War II*. Hurstpierpoint, West Sussex: The Dorothy L. Sayers Society, 2008.

———. "Christ the Worker." *The Catholic Herald*, April 18, 1941.

———. "The Christian Faith and the Theatre." MS. 43 n.d. The Marion E. Wade Center, Wheaton College, Wheaton, IL.

———. "The Church in the New Age." *World Review* (March 1941) 12–14.

———. "The Church's Responsibility." In *Malvern, 1941: The Life of the Church and the Order of Society*. London: Longmans, Green, 1941.

———. *Clouds of Witness*. London: Unwin, 1926.

———. *Creed or Chaos? and Other Essays in Popular Theology*. London: Methuen, 1947.

———. "Do Writers Work?" MS 69 n.d. The Marion E. Wade Center, Wheaton College, Wheaton, IL.

———. *The Documents in the Case*. With Robert Eustace. London: Ernest Benn, 1930.

———. "Eros in Academe." *The Oxford Outlook* (June 1919) 110–16.

———. *Even the Parrot Exemplary Conversations for Enlightened Children*. 2nd ed. London: Methuen, 1944.

———. *The Five Red Herrings*. London: Victor Gollancz, 1931.

———. *Four Sacred Plays*. London: Victor Gollancz, 1948.

———. *Gaudy Night*. London: Victor Gollancz, 1936.

———. "Gaudy Night." In *Titles to Fame* edited by Denys Kilham Roberts, 75–95. London: Nelson, 1937

———, editor, *Great Short Stories of Detection, Mystery and Horror First Series*. London: Victor Gollancz,1928.

———, editor. *Great Short Stories of Detection, Mystery and Horror Second Series*. London: Victor Gollancz, 1931.

———, editor. *Great Short Stories of Detection, Mystery and Horror Third Series*. London: Victor Gollancz, 1934.

———. *Hangman's Holiday*. London: Victor Gollancz, 1933.

———. *Have His Carcase*. London: Victor Gollancz, 1932.

———. "Is this He that Should Come?" *The Christian News-Letter*, 20 December, 1939 Supplement No. 8.

———. Letter File 296 n.d. The Marion E. Wade Center, Wheaton College, Wheaton, IL.

———. *The Letters of Dorothy L Sayers Volume 1 1899–1936 The Making of a Detective Novelist*. Edited by Barbara Reynolds. Hurstpierpoint, West Sussex: The Dorothy L. Sayers Society, 1995.

———. *The Letters of Dorothy L Sayers Volume 2 1937–1943 From Novelist to Playwright*. Edited by Barbara Reynolds. Hurstpierpoint, West Sussex: The Dorothy L. Sayers Society, 1997.

———. *The Letters of Dorothy L Sayers Volume 3 1944–1950 A Noble Daring*. Edited by Barbara Reynolds. Hurstpierpoint, West Sussex: The Dorothy L. Sayers Society, 1998.

———. *The Letters of Dorothy L Sayers Volume 4 1951–1957 In the Midst of Life*. Edited by Barbara Reynolds. Hurstpierpoint, West Sussex: The Dorothy L. Sayers Society, 2000.

———. *Lord Peter Views the Body*. London: Victor Gollancz, 1929.

———. *Lord Peter: A Collection of all the Lord Peter Wimsey Stories*. New York: Avon, 1972.

———. *Love All: Together with Busman's Honeymoon*. Edited by Alzina Dale. Kent State, OH: Kent State University Press. 1984

———. *Making Sense of the Universe.* Pamphlet. n.d.

———. *The Man Born To Be King.* 5th ed. London: Victor Gollancz, 1944.

———. *The Mind of the Maker.* New York: HarperCollins, 1987.

———. *Murder Must Advertise.* London: Victor Gollancz, 1933.

———. "My Edwardian Childhood" In *Dorothy L. Sayers Child and Woman of her Time,* edited by Barbara Reyolds, 1–24. Hurstpierpoint, West Sussex: The Dorothy L. Sayers Society, 2002.

———. "Nativity Play." *Radio Times,* December 23, 1938, 13.

———. *The Nine Tailors.* London: Victor Gollancz, 1934.

———. "Notes on the Way." *Time and Tide,* June 15, 1940, 634.

———. "Notes on the Way." *Time and Tide,* June 22, 1940, 657.

———. *Op I.* London: Longmans, Green, 1916.

———. "Playwrights are not Evangelists." *World Theatre* 5 (1955–56) 61–66.

———. "A Plea for Vocation in Work." *Bulletins from Britain* (August 19 1942) 7–10.

———. "Prevention is Better than Cure." *St. Martin's Review* (December 1939) 548.

———. "The Psychology of Advertising." *The Spectator* (November 19, 1937) 896–98.

———. *Strong Poison.* London: Ernest Benn, 1930.

———. "Trials and Sorrows of a Mystery Writer." *The Listener,* January 6, 1932.

———. *Tristan in Brittany.* Translated by Dorothy L. Sayers. London: Ernest Benn, 1929.

———. *Unnatural Death.* London: Ernest Benn, 1927.

———. *The Unpleasantness at the Bellona Club.* London: Ernest Benn, 1928.

———. *Unpopular Opinions.* London: Victor Gollancz, 1946.

———. "Vocation in Work." In *A Christian Basis for the Post-War World,* edited by A. E. Baker, 88–103. London: SCM, 1942.

———. "War and Post-War Screwtapery." MS 236 n.d. The Marion E. Wade Center, Wheaton College, Wheaton, IL.

———. "What is Man?" MS 237 n.d. The Marion E. Wade Center, Wheaton College, Wheaton, IL.

———. "The Wimsey Papers." *The Spectator* (November 17, 1939) 672–74.

———. "The Wimsey Papers II." *The Spectator* (November 24, 1939) 736–37.

———. "The Wimsey Papers III." *The Spectator* (December 1, 1939) 770–71.

———. "The Wimsey Papers IV." *The Spectator* (December 8, 1939) 809–10.

———. "The Wimsey Papers V." *The Spectator* (December 15, 1939) 859–60.

———. "The Wimsey Papers VI." *The Spectator* (December 22, 1939) 894–95.

———. "The Wimsey Papers VII." *The Spectator* (December 29, 1939) 925–26.

———. "The Wimsey Papers VIII." *The Spectator* (January 5, 1940) 8–9.

———. "Wimsey Papers IX." *The Spectator* (January 12, 1940) 38–39.

———. "The Wimsey Papers X." *The Spectator* (January 19, 1940) 70–71.

———. "The Wimsey Papers XI." *The Spectator* (January 26, 1940) 104–5.

———. *Whose Body?* London: T. Fisher Unwin, 1923.

———. *Why Work?* London: Methuen, 1942.

———. "Work" [Sword of the Spirit speech notes] MS 243 n.d. The Marion E. Wade Center, Wheaton College, Wheaton, IL.

Schwöbel, Christoph, editor. *Trinitarian Theology Today Essays on Divine Being and Act.* Edinburgh: T. & T. Clark, 1995.

Schwöbel, Christoph, and Colin E. Gunton, editors. *Persons Divine and Human.* Edinburgh: T. & T. Clark, 1991.

Sedgwick, Peter. "Christian Teaching on Work and the Economy." In *Unemployment and the Future of Work*, 219–28. London: Council of Churches for Britain and Ireland, 1997.

Sennett, Richard. *The Corrosion of Character: The Personal Consequences of Work in a New Capitalism*. London: Norton, 1998.

Soskice, Janice Martin. "Love and Attention." In *Philosophy, Religion and the Spiritual Life*, Royal Institute of Philosophy Supplement 32, edited by M. McGhee, 59–72. Cambridge: Cambridge University Press, 1992.

Suggate, Alan M. *William Temple and Christian Social Ethics Today*. Edinburgh: T. & T. Clark, 1987.

The Tablet. Editorial. May 17, 1941, 384.

———. Books of the Week: *Malvern 1941*. February 21, 1942, 100.

Temple, William. Correspondence with Dorothy L. Sayers. Lambeth Palace. Archive Vol. 39, ff. 227–80. n.d.

———. "Thomism and Modern Needs." *Blackfriars* (March 1944) 86–92. doi: 10.1111/j.1741-2005.1944.tb05673.x

Thompson, John. *Modern Trinitarian Perspectives*. Oxford: Oxford University Press, 1994.

Thurmer, John. *A Detection of the Trinity*. Exeter: Paternoster, 1984.

———. *Reluctant Evangelist Papers on the Christian Thought of Dorothy L. Sayers*. Hurstpierpoint, The Dorothy L. Sayers Society, 1996.

The Times. "Report on Oxford Conference on Church, Community and State." July 21, 1937, 9.

Tischler, Nancy. "Artist, Artifact, and Audience: The Aesthetics and Practice of Dorothy L. Sayers." In *As Her Whimsey Took Her: Critical Essays on the Work of Dorothy L. Sayers*, edited by Margaret P. Hannay, 153–64. Kent, OH: Kent State University Press, 1979.

Vann, G., OP. Review of *The Greatest Drama Ever Staged* by Dorothy L. Sayers. *Blackfriars* (August 1938) 627.

———. Review of *Begin Here* by Dorothy L. Sayers. *Blackfriars* (March 1940) 198.

———. Review of *The Mind of the Maker* by Dorothy L. Sayers. *Blackfriars* (October 1941) 562–63.

Walsh, Jill Paton. "The Immortal Lord Peter." Speech given at St. Ives Library, 30 March, 2004.

Walsh, Michael J. *From Sword to Ploughshare: Sword of the Spirit to Catholic Institute for International Relations 1940–1980*. London: Catholic Institute for International Relations, 1980.

Watson, Giles. "The Oecumenical Penguin." *VII An Anglo-American Literary Review* 14. Wheaton, IL: The Marion E. Wade Center, 1997, 17–32.

Welch, Claude. *The Trinity in Contemporary Theology*. London: SCM, 1953.

White, Victor, OP, STL. "Tasks for Thomists. Some Reflections on 'Thomism and Modern Needs' by His Grace the Archbishop of Canterbury." *Blackfriars* (March 1944) 93–117.

Williams, Rowan. *Anglican Identities*. London: Darton Longman & Todd, 2004.

Woodruff, Douglas. "For Christian Civilization." *The Tablet* (February 17, 1940) 156.

———. Review of *The Zeal of thy House* by Dorothy L. Sayers. *Punch* (April 6, 1938) 384.

Zizioulas, J. D. "The Doctrine of the Holy Trinity: The Significance of the Cappadocian Contribution." In *Trinitarian Theology Today Essays on Divine Being and Act*, edited by Christoph Schwöbel, 44–60. Edinburgh: T. & T. Clark, 1995.

————. "On Being a Person: Towards an Ontology of Personhood." In *Persons Divine and Human*, edited by Christoph Schwöbel and Colin Gunton, 33–46. Edinburgh: T. & T. Clark, 1991.

Index

Abdication Crisis, 33
Address to undergraduates, 104
After Virtue, 93, 107, 113, 115
Anglican Social Ethics, ix, xx, 39, 57,
    58–69, 93
    criticism of, 60–61
    history of, 58–69
Anglican philosophy, 58
Anglicanism, self-understanding,
    59, 62
Anglo-Catholics, 64
Anthony, Peter D., 102
Anthropology, xi, 70
    of autonomous individual, 79, 88
        115, 117
    of man as sinner, 59
    Marxist, 87
    relationality, 88–89
    Sayers' Trinitarian anthropology,
        xviii, 55–56, 60, 71–72, 83–
        90, 93, 94, 113, 120, 121
    single nature, 76, 84
    two-nature, 76, 83, 87,
    theological, xvii–xviii, xx, 63, 65,
        78, 79, 80–83, 85, 86, 92
Archbishops' Commission on Church
    and State, 59
"Are Women Human?," 44, 83
"Art: A Trinitarian perspective," 81
"Aristotle on Detective Fiction," 18
Armstrong, Walter H., 52, 124

Artist, xix, 37, 43, 45, 50, 55, 73, 76,
    78, 79, 88, 89, 95
    values, 21–22, 35, 108
    way of working, 55, 100, 106
    artistic integrity, 103–5
    assembly line, 92, 101
Athanasius, 32
Athanasian Creed, xvi, 1–2, 7, 77
Atonement, 36, 37, 44
Augustine, Saint, xx, 74–75, 79, 90
autonomous individual *see* person in
    modernity
autonomy
    of secular sciences, 65
    of secular vocation, 66, 106
Avarice, 53, 116

Babingdon, Margaret, 7
Barth, Karl, 61, 63, 67, 76
Barthianism, 60
BBC, 8, 9, 32, 41, 44, 47n22, 51, 57
Beales, A. C., 52
Bedoyère, Count Michael de la, 56
Begin Here, 9, 42, 48, 52, 70, 83, 84,
    92
Bell, George, 52, 54, 56, 62, 67
Benson's Advertising Agency, 5, 6, 29
Berdyaev, Nicholas, 68
Berry, Sidney, 54
Blackfriars, 48, 75
Blackwell, Basil, 4

Blitz, 52, 54
Bloomsbury, 20, 21
Bolton, Roger and Dorothy G., 119
Book of Common Prayer, 1
Bouquet, Rev., 67
Borne, Etienne, 95
Brabazon, James, 6n18, 10, 11
British Council of Churches, 79
Broadcast Minds, 66
Brown, David, 78–79
Brunner, Emil, 68
bureaucracy
    and institutions, 94, 115
    Sayers' criticism of, 116, 119, 121
Busman's Honeymoon, xvi, 6, 7, 18,
        19, 21, 23, 28, 32–34
Byrne, Muriel St Clair, 32, 33

Campbell, Canon, 67
Canterbury, 7, 37, 38
Canterbury Festival, 7, 9, 16, 32, 34,
        43, 44
Cappadocian fathers, 80
Catholic Herald, 54, 56
Catholic Tales and Christian Songs, 4,
        14, 26
Catholic Writers Guild, 10, 58
Challenge of the Slums, The, 62
Chesterton, Gilbert Keith, 3, 67
Christ of the Creeds, 51
Christendom group, 62, 63, 64–65, 66,
        93, 100
Christian Crisis, 56
"Christian Faith and the Theatre,
        The," 31
Christian Newsletter, 46, 50, 54, 58
Christian Social Union, 62, 64
Christianity, 3, 45, 46, 49, 73
    Creeds, 40, 41, 45
    doctrine as intellectual
        framework, 49, 57
    ignorance of, 42–44
Christie, Agatha, 14, 19
Christology, 11, 47
Chub, Margaret, 2
Church, 52–53, 90, 95
    and arts 53, 105–6

and politics, 52, 53, 90
and secular vocation, 105–6
"Church in the New Age, The," 85
Church Times, 48, 54–55
"Church's Responsibility, The," 52
Churchill, Winston, 50
Clouds of Witness, 5
Collingwood, R. G., 17
Collins, Wilkie, 18
common good in liberal capitalism,
        115, 117
communion, 80, 82, 83, 90
Communism, 42, 48, 61, 92, 125
Community, 80, 87, 109, 113, 119,
        121
    in Sayers' detective fiction, 18, 29
    and work, 56
Commonweal, 75
confessing Church, 61
consumer, 114, 116
consumerism, 121
COPEC Interdenominational
        Conference on Politics,
        Economics and Citizenship,
        60, 62
Cournos, John, 5, 11
Courtly love, 12–14, 27, 29
Covetousness, 116
Craftsmanship, 104, 106
Creation, 95
creative mind, 15, 45, 71, 73
creativity, 72, 76, 78, 80, 81, 87, 120,
        121
creator,
    analogy between human and
        divine 36
    divine, 43
    as metaphor, 74
Creed or Chaos?, book 14, 40
    BBC talks 51
    speech, 48–49, 50, 52, 85
Crockford's Clerical Directory, 64, 66
Crucifixion, 38, 45

D'Arcy, Fr Martin SJ, 54
Dante, xix, 10, 11, 57
Davidson, Randall, 58

Dawson, Christopher, 52, 54
Demant, V. A., 48, 50n32, 62n82, 105
Dependent Rational Animals, xviii, 88, 107, 110
Depression, 60
Determinists, 42
Devil to Pay, The, 9
Distributivists, 93, 100
Divine Comedy, 10–11, 12–13
Documents in the Case, The, 6, 22
dogma, 7, 8, 32, 38, 41, 42, 43, 44, 47, 49, 54, 55, 59, 61, 63, 66, 73, 82, 87, 125–26
Downside Review, 75
Doyle, Conan, 17
Drucker, Peter, 48, 92, 101–2, 119
Dublin Review, 75
Dulles, Avery SJ, 80, 81
Dunkirk, 50

Eastbourne, 54, 55, 56
ecclesiology, 52–53, 63
economic man, 48, 70
ecumenism, 46, 52, 54–57
    difficulties of, 56
    and social ethics, 39, 61, 68
    and Trinity, 78, 80
Edinburgh Conference on Faith and Order, 60, 61
Edwards, Ruth Dudley, 26
Eliot, T. S., 50n32, 57
Emperor Constantine, The, 11, 14
End of Economic Man, The, 48, 92
ENERGY, second term of Sayers' analogy, 14, 30, 38, 45, 71, 73, 75, 76, 89, 90, 125
Envy, 116
eros, 12,
    as 'passionate politics' 25
    "Eros in Academe," 4, 11, 12
Eustace, Robert, 6
existentialism, 70, 79

faith, 3
    intellectual, 40
    emotional, 40
Fall, the, 48, 86, 94

Family, xvi, 17, 20, 63, 70, 86, 90, 94, 117, 123, 124
    family wage, 62n82, 93
    as practice, xviii, xx, 90, 107, 112, 113, 120
    in social ethics, 82, 119, 120
    Wimsey family, 24, 47
fan vs consumer, 114
Fascism, 42, 48, 61, 92
Faust, 9
Feminism
    difference, 86
    equity, 70
    Second Wave, xv, 86
    welfare, 70
Fenn, Rev. Eric, 51
Five Red Herrings, 6, 21
"Food for the Full Grown," 45
Forgotten Trinity, The, 79
Fornication, 53
Frankenberg, Claris, 2
free love, 20, 24
free will, 75
    Further Papers on Dante, 11

Galatians 3:2, 884
Galot, 79
Garbett, Cyril, 62
Gaudy Night, xv, xvi, 6, 18, 23, 25–28, 33, 34
gender, 70–71, 82, 90
    equality, xvii, 32, 38, 55, 70–71, 81–82, 84, 120
    roles, xv, 2, 13–14, 82, 110, 117, 120
    separate spheres, 91, 92, 94, 112, 117, 120
    stereotypes, 18, 19, 27–28, 29, 33–34, 38, 44, 71, 84, 94, 110, 112, 120
    and work, xvii, xviii, xx, 9, 14, 16, 55, 90, 94, 111–13, 120
Genesis
    1:27   84
    2:15   125
    3:19   125
Gill, Eric, 95

Index

Godolphin School, 2
Gollancz, Victor, 9, 48, 104
good product, 99, 102–4
    goods of practices, 108, 109, 115, 121
Gospels, 3, 89
Great Short Stories of Detection, Mystery and Horror, 7
"Greatest Drama, The," 8, 42, 48, 49
Greene, Oswald, 5
guilds, 63, 66, 69
Gunton, Colin E., 79, 80

Haack, Susan, 84n52, 86–87
Hangman's Holiday, 6
Hastings, Adrian, 60, 62
Hauerwas, Stanley, xviii
Have His Carcase, 6, 23, 25
"He That Should Come," 8, 46
Heenan, John, 40
Heilbrun, Carolyn, 12
Henry, François, 95
Hinsley, Arthur, 51, 52, 54, 56, 68, 124
Hodgson, Leonard, 4, 77
homo faber, 71, 87
honesty, 104
Horlicks, 104
Horne, Brian, 81
"Human–Not–Quite–Human, The," 83

IDEA, Sayers' analogue for the Father, 30, 36, 37, 38, 71, 73, 75, 76, 89, 90
Ideology of Work, The, 102
image of God, 32, 79
    in ability to create, 45, 55, 66, 71, 74, 87, 125
    in capacity for God, 89–90
    in relationality, 80
Incarnation, xvi, 7–8, 14–15, 32, 34, 36, 38, 43, 47, 53, 56, 59, 68, 69, 81, 82, 126
independent practical reasoners, 107, 110–11, 112

Industrial Christian Fellowship, 49, 62
Ingram, Sir Richard, 50n32, 64
Inklings, 10
Institutions, 115, 117, 121; *see* bureaucracy
integration, 101–2
intellectual corruption, 53
intellectual integrity, 25–26
intellectual sloth, 53
Introductory Papers on Dante, 11
Iremonger, F. A., 8
"Is this He that should come?," 46

Jesuanists, 42, 47
Job design, Sayers' prescription for, 55, 99, 100, 101, 121; *see* integration
Joint Letter, 52, 61, 123–24
judgment, 50
Just Vengeance, The, xix, 11, 14, 88

Kelly, Herbert Hamilton, 7, 40
Kenney, Catherine, 17, 26
Knox, Ronald, 58, 66

LaCugna, Catherine M., 78, 79, 80, 81, 82
Lambeth D.D., 57
Lang, Cosmo, 52, 54–55, 67, 124
League of Nations, 60
Leigh, Mabel, 6
leisure, 55, 95–99, 114
Lewis, C. S., 103
Ley, Henry, 4
Lindbeck, George, xviii
    Loades, Ann, xviii, 84
Lord Peter Views the Body, 6
Love All, 9, 18, 32, 34, 44
Love and Attention, 111
Lyon, Hugh, 54

MacIntyre, Alasdair, x, xviii, 72, 80, 88, 89, 90, 93, 94, 106–21
    and capitalism, 93–94, 114, 115
    practices, 107–12, 114

virtues of acknowledged
dependency, 94, 111, 112
McLaughlin, Patrick, 10, 57, 58
Making Sense of the Universe, 57
Malvern Conference, ix, 49–50, 52,
53, 57, 58, 60, 62, 63–64, 66,
67, 69, 71
Man Born To Be King, The, xvii, xix,
9, 14, 15
Managers,
character of, 119
knowledge claims of, 115
Maritain, Jacques, 68
Margaret of Navarre, 13
Marriage, 18, 20–24, 27, 29, 33, 34
Martin, Francis, 81
Mascall, Eric L., 78, 79, 82
materialists, 42
Matricide at St Martha's, 26
Men Without Work, 62
Middle Axioms, 65
Middlemore, Amphilis, 2
Milton, John, 76
Mind of the Maker, The, ix, xvii, xix,
7, 9, 15, 26, 29, 31–32, 43, 45,
48, 51, 56, 71–77, 87, 96, 116
Mind of the Maker, The [book
review], 75–76
Moberly, Walter, 62
money, 50
Moot, 10
Murder Must Advertise, 6, 16, 23, 29,
31, 74, 104
Murray, John, SJ, 52
Mustard Club, 5
Mutual Admiration Society, 2
Mystical Body, 87

Narrative theology, 9
Nativity play, 46
natural law, 39, 58, 59,62, 63, 65, 69,
90, 108, 119
natural theology, 58, 62–63
Nazism, 60, 66, 68
Niebuhr, Reinhold, 61, 65, 67, 68
Nine Tailors, The, 6, 15, 23, 29, 47,
104

O'Neill, Mary Aquin, 82–83, 84n52
O'Sullivan, Richard Q. C., 54
Oecumenical Penguin, 56–57, 68
Oldham, Dr. J. H., 10, 46, 50, 54, 62
Op I, 4
Oxford Conference on Church,
Community and State, 60–62
Oxford University, 3–4, 26

Paget, Francis, 58
person in modernity, 79, 88
personal responsibility, 9, 38, 40,
41–42, 47, 118
personhood, 80, 88
Philosophy of Work, A, 95
phoney war, 46
Pilgrim Trust, 62
Pius XII, Pope, 52
*Poetry of Search and the Poetry of
Statement, The*, 11
Pope, Mildred, 2, 6
posivitist philosophy, 70
post–war reconstruction, 39–40, 48
pot boilers, 104
POWER, Sayers' analogue for the
Holy Spirit, 30, 31, 38, 71, 73,
75, 76, 77, 87, 88, 89, 90
practices, xx, 94, 107–10, 112
Preston, Ronald, 64–65, 66, 68
"Prevention is better than Cure," 46
Pride, 12, 35–37, 53, 89
private property, 64, 65
problem/solution mentality, 51,
96–97, 116
profit motive, 61, 64
Purgatory, 12–13

Quadragesimo Anno, 93
Quick, Oliver Chase, 56–57, 68

Radical Orthodoxy, x
Radio Times, 8
Rahner, Karl SJ, 78
Ramsey Michael, 58, 59, 67–68
rational consumer, 111
Rathbone, Eleanor, 70
Ratzinger, Joseph, 74–75

Index

Raven, Charles, 60, 76
Rawlinson, Alfred Edward John, 48
Reckitt, Maurice, 19, 50n32, 62n82
    redemption, 33, 36, 50, 68
relationality, 37, 80–83, 87, 88, 118–9
Religious Prospect, The, 48
Rerum Novarum, 93
resurrection, 37, 38, 45, 58, 59
Reynolds, Barbara, 7, 9
Rowe, Dorothy, 2

Sacramental view of universe, xviii,
    14–15, 32, 39, 40, 48, 55–56,
    66, 94, 126
Sayers, Dorothy Leigh
    criticism of, 66–67
    detective fiction, xix, 16–38
    ecclesiology, 52–53, 63
    evaluation of, 65
    faith, 3, 9, 11, 14, 17–18, 42, 89
    personal life, marriage, son, 2–6,
        10, 11–12, 17
    and theater, xx, 7, 9, 31–32, 37,
        57, 89
    theological method, xvii, xix, 8,
        40–42, 57, 63, 69, 72–73
    work experiences, xx, 4–6, 14
Sayers, Helen Mary, 6, 67
Sayers, Henry, 1, 6
Scholastic philosophy, 40
Scholastics, 63
Schwöbel, Christoph, 78, 79
Sennett, Richard, 102
Sexton Blake novels, 4
Shaw, Gilbert, 10, 57
Shrimpton, Ivy, 6
Simpson, Wallis, 33
Sin, 41, 49, 65
social contract theory, 116
Socialism, 48, 59, 93
solidarity in guilt, 18, 33, 42–43
Somerville College, 2, 25
Song of Roland, The, 10
Soskice, Janice Martin, 111
Spectator, 46–47, 75
St. Anne's, Soho, 10, 57, 58
Stoll Theater, 54

Strong Poison, 6, 21, 22–23
Sunday Times, 7–8, 40, 42, 45
superfluous women, 19, 22
Sword of the Spirit, 51–52, 54, 56

Tablet, 48, 55, 75
Talbot, Neville, 41
Tanks for Russia, 100
Taylorism, 92, 101
Temple, William, x, xx, 39, 46, 49,
        50n32, 51, 52, 56–57, 58–69,
        124
    ecumenical leader, 60
    social ethics, 59, 60, 63, 64, 65
    theology, 59, 63, 65
theology of crisis, 60, 67
Thomas Aquinas, Saint, x, 65, 89
Thomism, 65, 67
Three Musketeers, The, 17
Thurmer, John, 76, 89
Tillich, Paul, 61
Time and Tide, 50, 57
Times (London), 44, 52, 54, 61, 123
Tischler, Nancy, 89
Titles to Fame, 18, 22–23, 25
totalitarianism, 62, 92; *see also*
        Communism, Fascism,
        Nazism
Trinity, xvi, 7, 15, 29, 32, 34, 37, 38,
        43–44, 56, 69, 72–73, 76–83
    Sayers' analogy for, xvii, xviii, xx,
        7, 9, 16, 29–32, 32, 37, 38, 45,
        71, 73–75, 76, 90
Tristan in Brittany, 6, 13
"Triumph of Easter, The," 42–43, 49

Unemployment, 61, 69, 92, 93
unions, 93
Unnatural Death, 6, 19, 21
Unpleasantness at the Bellona Club,
    The, 6, 20–21
Unpopular Opinions, 40
"Unsolved Puzzle of the Man with No
    Face, The," 21–22

Vane, Harriet, xvi, 14, 18, 22, 23–29,
        33, 34, 47

Vann, Gerald OP, 48, 75
Virgin Birth, 58–59
"Vocation in Work," 87
vocation. *See* Work, vocation in

Walsh, Jill Paton, 16
Walsh, Michael J., 54
Ward, Barbara, 52, 54
Welch, Claude, 77
Welch, James, 51, 56, 57, 68
"What do we believe?," 45
What is Man?, 84–86
Whelpton, Eric, 4, 11
"When All the Saints," 4
White, William, 5
"Who Calls the Tune?," 2
Whose Body?, 5, 23, 26
Why Work?, 55, 106
Williams, Charles, 7, 10, 57
Williams, Harcourt, 38
Williams, Rowan, 59
"Wimsey Papers, The," 47
Wimsey, Lord Peter, ix, xvi, xx, 1, 5,
    6, 14, 18, 19, 20–29, 33, 34,
    38, 47, 54, 104
  work, 23–24, 33, 38
Wimsey-Vane relationship, 14, 22,
    23–29, 32, 33–34, 83
Witham, 6, 58

Work, x, xviii, 9, 34, 55, 57, 120
  of care, xviii, 84, 90, 110–11,
    112–13
  in Christian tradition, 91, 94–95
  conditions of, 91–93, 120
  craftsmanship, 104
  duty to serve the work, 104–5,
    121
  good work, 22, 94, 99–100, 109,
    112, 126
  integrity in, xvi, 9, 25–26, 28, 29,
    32, 33–36, 66, 94
  and leisure, 55, 95–96
  to live or live to work, 97–98
  as part of practice, 109, 112
  theology of x, 16, 56, 76, 120,
    125–26
  as toil, 91, 94, 100
  in Wimsey-Vane courtship, 28
  and vocation, 9, 14, 34–38, 54–56,
    105, 118, 120, 124, 125–26
  women's, xv, 12, 19–20, 25, 91–92
World Council of Churches, 61
Writing a Woman's Life, 12
Zeal of thy House, The, xvii, xix, 7,
    12, 16, 26, 29, 34–38, 42, 43,
    71, 104
Zizioulas, J. D., 80